Sports Marketing

"The Money Side of Sports"

By Kermit Pemberton

Sports Services of America Publishing™
333 Washington Blvd., Suite 360
Marina Del Rey, CA 90292

This book is dedicated to the Boys & Girls Clubs of America,
which keep many of America's youth in between the lines instead
of out on the streets.

Sports Marketing: "The Money Side of Sports"

Sports Services of America Publishing™
333 Washington Blvd., Suite 360
Marina Del Rey, CA 90292
(310) 821-4490

Copyright © 1997 by Sports Services of America Publishing™

Include bibliographical references and index.

ISBN 0-9656421-9-4

This book is available at special discounts when purchased in bulk quantities for businesses, associations, institutions, or sales promotions. Please contact Kermit Pemberton at (310) 821-4490.

Special thanks to K. T. "Jaguar's" assistant editor, DeAnne Steele, a UCLA graduate in English who is now entering The Anderson Graduate School of Management at UCLA, and to Dianna Brotarlo for assistance in editing this book.

AUTHOR: KERMIT PEMBERTON

Kermit Pemberton is a professional speaker and has over 13 years combined experience in sports marketing. He was introduced to the sports industry during the Olympic Games in the summer of 1984 in Los Angeles. Since then, he has organized annual sporting programs to some for the world's greatest sporting events, including the Super Bowl, Final Four, Pro Bowl, World Series and U.S. Open (Golf and Tennis). He has traveled around the world to a total of six Olympics, both winter and summer. He has forged lasting corporate relationships with clients such as Hitachi, 1-800-COLLECT, Owens Corning Fiberglass, Images USA Marketing, and Sports Tours Classic. His goal is to educate all about professional sports and the promotion of health and fitness in America.

SPECIAL GUEST WRITER: K.T. "JAGUAR" MYERS

It was at Muskingum College in New Concord, Ohio, that he took on the name "Jaguar" as Sports Director for 90.7 WMCO. Jaguar is currently the editor for many sports publications. He lent his smooth writing and editing style to the creation of this book. Jaguar captures sports from the fans' perspective, since he is in the business of serving the fans and keeping their interest. Kermit Pemberton writes from his interest and knowledge of the business side of sports. Together with the help of many others, they have created *Sports Marketing: "The Money Side of Sports."*

TABLE OF CONTENTS

VII

Endorsements

"This is a must-read book for any student, instructor, or person looking to expand knowledge in sports marketing. Step-by-step outlines and real-life examples of sports promotions are the key to learning how to tie in professional sports with products and services."

-Scott Williams
Images Marketing Firm

"I now realize the reason why over 90% of potential clients that I take to a sporting event end up as clients. Sports encompasses the association of work ethic, loyalty, community support, goodwill, family, commitment, and of course winning and success. Thank you for all the excellent game tickets you have provided us with throughout the years. I have truly never seen a book on sports marketing with so many real hands-on examples of sports promotions and programs."

-Gary Hatfield
Owens Corning Fiberglass

"To express very simply, this is the best book ever written on sports marketing!"

-Joy Kenel
Marketing Plus Events

"I am truly amazed at how interesting the business side of sports is. Over $26 billion are spent on health and fitness theme events. Over $40 million in endorsements for Michael Jordan. One million dollars to buy luxury skyboxes per year. I am also amazed at the main reason why fans

associate with teams . This book will be a bestseller. I give this book nine stars!"

-James Baldwin
Bookworld Review

"This book reads very well and is so interesting to the everyday, hardworking sports fan. I am your number-one fan! You have hit a grand slam with this book."

-Priscilla Pemberton
Mother and sports fan

"This is the best sports marketing book I have ever read. A must-read for anybody associated with the business side of sports."

-James Wilson
Sport Agent Consultant

"With only 60,000 people watching a game live, I was amazed to find out that millions of dollars are being spent on media coverage, sponsorship, and merchandise."

-George Radcliff
Sports fan

"Finally, a book with examples written by someone with years of experience who talks and relates directly to me. The examples of endorsement deals and terms are excellent. I wonder if Michael Jordan would endorse my flower shop, since they expect him to sell over $200 million worth of cologne? I now know different deals and percentages that I can approach athletes with. I wonder if Mike can do the same for my flower shop!"

-Nancy Freedman
California Sunshine Flowers

Chapter 1

Sports Marketing

Sports marketing is the selling of sports, whether you are promoting the NBA – by such means as their slogan, "NBA Action is Fantastic" – or comparing two athletes going head to head – Michael Jordan vs. Magic Johnson – or two teams opposing each other; the 1996 Super Bowl featured the Pittsburgh Steelers against the Dallas Cowboys, eliciting NFL tradition by comparing these two teams to their counterparts from the 1976 and 1979 Super Bowls, respectively. Reebok and Nike market themselves by using high-profile athletes to endorse their products. They also use sponsorships to secure associations with teams or players – Nike and the Dallas Cowboys, or Reebok and Dallas Cowboy running back Emmitt Smith. These are examples of sports marketing. Billions of dollars are spent each year marketing sports and marketing through sports. Any attempt to promote a product or service through a sport, an athlete, or an aspect of a game is sports marketing.

Corporations and sports organizations have developed a unique relationship. In the past, the most popular athletes were used by corporations as pitch men. Teams sold broadcast rights, and the majority of revenue was limited to individual teams, souvenir dealers, and leagues.

Corporate America and sports have since teamed up to create mutually beneficial revenue arrangements. Businesses now design advertising and sales campaigns around sports and sports figures. Corporations view sports as vehicles for corporate advertising, sponsorship, and expansion. The role of sports and the role of business have grown together. Corporate monetary contributions to sports are broken down into the following percentage categories:

- **30% is consumed by sales promotion.**

- **30% is spent on luxury suites, tickets and other hospitality-related expenses for clients.**

- **15% is spent on television advertising.**

- **15% is spent on advertising space in newspapers, magazines, and programs.**

- **10% goes toward sponsor fees.**

Corporate America is also represented in the 1995 *Sporting News* annual list of the "100 Most Powerful" people in sports, which included: General Motors' Donald Zarrella and Philip Gurarascio;

Coca Cola's Charles Fruit; Anheuser-Busch's Tony Ponturo; McDonald's Paul Schrage; David D'Alessandro and John Hancock; and Microsoft's Bill Gates. These men represent the relationship between big business and sports.

Sports are a part of American culture and the American public is constantly exposed to sports in one form or another. The growth of sports radio – and more importantly, television – illustrates America's love for sports. In 1987, Americans watched sporting events approximately 574 million times. ESPN reached more than 66 million homes. That is roughly 61% of all the households in the U.S. with television sets. In 1990, there were approximately 7,500 hours of sports programming on cable stations and networks. ESPN increased its hours of sports events programming from 2,700 in 1980 to nearly 4,500 in 1990, nearly doubling in a decade.

Sports marketing can be considered an event itself, with new products, athlete endorsements, and combative efforts by companies looking to outdo their opponents. It's a crazy thing. Commercials have now become events and promotions. On the field of athlete tie-ins, companies hustle to get the most well-known sports figures to endorse their shoes, and BAM! – anything goes. Billions of dollars are spent, all for market-share, all for money. The skill and excitement of sports marketing makes it similar to the NBA, NFL, NHL, and MLB. Instead of players pitted against each other, though, it's Nike vs. Reebok. And it's far more competitive today than ever before.

Sports interest increases yearly. If you measure the attendance and television ratings, you will begin to understand the business potency of sports. That is why corporations now look to sports to promote products and services. The marketing of sports has been so extensive and successful, corporations look to model their own successes using sports. The industry goes beyond professional sports, college sports, and extreme sports. The Olympics have grown in attendance, and TV ratings are at an all-time high. Professional sports are more popular than ever. Entrepreneurial ventures between sports and business go well beyond media. They include sports properties, licensing, apparel, broadcast rights, and sponsorship of sporting events, teams, and stadiums. All generate incredible revenues.

Advantages of sports marketing for a company, league, or team include the generation of media attention, advertising, and public exposure that can reach a large group. The potential consumers in this large group have one thing in common – sports. The crowds can be quite large. A sporting event attracts people of all races, colors, and creeds together into one arena. In 1989-1990, six of the 10 most-watched TV shows were sporting events. Of the 10 highest-rated television programs of all time, five have been Super Bowl telecasts. Over 140 million people will watch the next Super

Bowl. A 30-second ad during the 1997 Super Bowl had a starting cost of $1.2 million.

Do You Remember Super Bowl XXVII?

A day-after telephone survey of 1,000 subjects by Cramer-Krasselt revealed how successful the retention of advertising was from the game, with a total commercial recall of 66% – a figure three times the "Big 3" networks' prime-time average day-after recall of only 23%. In the past, spots for Super Bowl XXVI had only a 59% recall, and the previous four Super Bowls were only 57%. Super Bowl XXVII's higher average was attributed to longer spots and to commercials with a continuation format.

If you do remember Super Bowl XXVII, you were among the millions of members viewing who watched the Dallas Cowboys hammer the Buffalo Bills 52-17 and made that game TV's most-watched program ever. Thirty-second spots for advertisers of the event sold for $850,000, which was another record. But even though the game was a blowout, viewers did not turn to their remote controls even when Dallas was assured the victory. Ratings did not drop significantly when the game's outcome was inevitable.

Even though the game may have been less exciting than fans hoped, viewers know they can see the best of advertising during Super Bowls. According to Performance Research, the highest-recalled advertiser was Pepsi at 49%, and the most liked spots were McDonald's and Lee Jeans, each at 15%. Additionally, a Nexis search of major newspapers showed that there were 98 mentions of Super Bowl XXVII advertisers in newspaper publications that game day. Nike had the highest mention frequency with 33, followed by Pepsi with 30, McDonald's with 28, Frito-Lay with 21, and Anheuser-Busch with 18.

Finally, viewers have been watching more commercials than actual football playing time in Super Bowls. In Super Bowl XXVII, playing time from kickoff to the final gun accounted for less than 10% of the total broadcast (15 minutes and 42 seconds), while commercials alone occupied nearly three times as much of the telecast as the plays (43 minutes and 30 seconds). Dead-ball time (huddles, measurements, and half-time activities) encompassed the remainder of the broadcast with 2 hours, 23 minutes, and 53 seconds. (COMPILED BY TRACY L. SCHOENADEL - SPORT INFORMATION SYSTEMS)

It was reported in 1989 that sports participation in the United States was shifting away from team sports toward more passive and individual sports. Swimming, exercise walking, and bicycle riding were the three most popular sports, while volleyball, baseball, basketball, and football were slightly declining. Was this reflected by television audiences? The trend at that time was correct. In 1991 baseball ratings were down 27%, and NFL broadcast ratings decreased 12%. However, new leagues, women's sports, and 24-hour access to sports information have changed the way we understand sports. In 1996, sports participation and TV ratings increased, bringing team sports into the forefront. The amount of money being spent merchandising team sports indicates this growth.

The popularity of sports is not measured solely by television ratings, but also by apparel. In 1990, sports properties totaled $10 billion. Licensed goods totaled 15% of sales. On the retail level, sales increased 7.5% overall in that same year.

Expansion teams, such as the Jacksonville Jaguars, have tremendous marketing potential. The NFL estimated that $30 million of Jaguar merchandise was sold in the first five days after the announcement that the team was being created. The retail success was largely attributed to the relationship between licensees and retailers. The two worked closely together to make sure the merchandise came out in a timely manner. Plans included product distribution, retail marketing, publicity, and advertising campaigns through print, outdoor and radio media.

Another revenue source is the licensing of broadcasts of sporting events to the media. The two primary sources are network television and cable television. Networks can profit from sportscasts by selling advertising and sponsorship time in the form of commercials promoting products and services.

One of the bolder moves in the sports coverage battle came when the Fox Broadcasting network outbid CBS for the rights to broadcast the National Football League (NFL), and the National Football Conference (NFC).

Fox Broadcasting Co. is gambling on the National Football Conference games to boost its ratings. After snagging the rights to cover the sporting events from CBS, this fourth largest network is aggressively marketing the games through billboards, radio, cable, newspapers, magazines, and in-theater commercial spots. Another facet of the promotional campaign is a multimillion-dollar watch-and-win cross promotion with McDonald's, which involves new advertisements featuring two die-hard fans. Fox officials are also touting their intention to provide the games with an attitude reflective of the network's image. Moreover, they have lowered the prices of advertisement spots and guaranteed high network ratings to win over advertisers.

Will Fox score a major touchdown with the addition of NFL football to its roster, or will the move go down as a major fumble for the fledgling fourth network?

On the surface, Fox's hip, young audience would seem to clash with the traditional older, male football viewer. But Fox says it hopes to cross over, exposing football fans to the likes of "Melrose Place" and turning its core audience of teens and young men and women on to gridiron action.

So far, sports marketing experts and advertisers seem to be giving Fox a fighting chance. Fox is less conservative than the more established networks and may even bring some new ideas to an old sport. In launching its football coverage, Fox claims to have undertaken the most aggressive multimedia marketing campaign in the history of sports. The tag for Fox NFL Sunday is "Same Game... New Attitude." The games will be presented in a form the audience is comfortable with, a Fox spokesman said, but with an attitude that reflects the network's edge.

The NFL deal gives Fox a big marketing platform to promote its prime-time programming. At the same time, Fox affiliates are promoting football through spots intended to make stars of Fox broadcasters and NFL players alike. Promos feature Fox Sports talent. (MARKETING NEWS 1994)

Since this took place, Fox has become the most aggressive sports network, including coverage of the 1996 World Series, and although the ratings for the World Series were low, they were Fox's highest ratings ever.

In 1995, Rupert Murdock of Fox was named the most powerful man in sports for the second year. He has led the way with Fox Sports, not necessarily looking at the short run, but always concentrating on the long run. In the future, Fox may become the sports leader. The network uses aggressive marketing for the NFL, including the talents of Terry Bradshaw, Howie Long, and James Brown. Besides football, Fox has worked out deals with Major League Baseball and the National Hockey League, along with a broadcast deal with Mike Tyson.

Before the mid '80s, it seemed as if the point of marketing sports was to increase ticket sales. Then leagues began to understand that there is more money to be made in sports than what is available through gate receipts. Tickets are not as profitable – and are in fact almost unimportant – when compared to television revenues, product endorsements, licensing and broadcast rights. Marketing efforts have gone way beyond ticket sales.

Licensing has become a big business in sports. Licensing involves more than just professional team apparel, but college apparel as well. On the college level, the NCAA authorizes merchandise using the NCAA logo. Items for the Final Four, the Collegiate World Series and all division championships require NCAA approval. Cross-licensing exists between the NCAA and individual universities with participating sports programs. International Collegiate Enterprises, an independent licensing agent, represents some universities and bowl games. Organizations such as the NCAA and International Collegiate Enterprises have the authority to authorize the licensing programs. Licensed apparel on any level is a form of marketing that promotes sports teams through increased visibility.

Why Do People Participate In Sports?

The thrill of victory, the agony of defeat, the underdog and the upset. Sports embodies passion and promotes fitness, health, and teamwork. Sports creates myths, legends, heroes, and failures. The world of sports is larger than life – a constant drive to be the best. The greatest men and women illustrate what it means to possess passion and heart. Sports is a real-life drama in an ever-changing environment. It allows an athlete to become a goat one night and a hero the next. Defeat has put the greatest athletes in tears when at the mercy of their opponents. The champion stands alone.

At the end of a grueling battle, only one is still standing. In order for one to endure greatness, a price must be paid: blood, sweat, and tears; overcoming the odds. One must reach deep down within the soul to find that greatness. For some of us, it's a lonely basketball court in the rain. For others, it is chanting, "3-2-1" as we launch the game winner and celebrate. Even if we don't share that moment with our team, there is still the affirmation of life – the greatness within. For almost everyone, there is one perfect moment that seems to overshadow every other.

Sports is very much a part of our culture and life. Sports captures the human spirit. There is no script to follow. Nail-biting games come down to the final seconds, or the last at-bat. Sports embodies the beauty of life. Those who have endured games on any level understand the commitment to excellence and the measure of heart and desire demanded by sports. People who are not gifted with great talent sometimes succeed against those with more. Athletes who suffer injuries sometimes come back against great odds. It is sheer desire, focus, and determination that drives sports.

Even the most unlikely hero or athlete has a story. Sports can be the most life-affirming experience one knows. Teamwork and victory measure the soldier within, and a constant physical and mental struggle underlies the battle on the field or court. Sports can be poetic and symbolic. Sports promotes teamwork and strength. Sports is about learning to trust your teammates – fight them, but more importantly, trust them. There can only be one goal: victory. Defeat can eat away at your heart and break you. In an individual's times of doubt, character can be defined. It brings the rush of adrenaline, the beating of your heart. It is feeling the passion, tension, and intensity of one moment when the world can be the most perfect place. One moment we stand in the spotlight, hoping our 15 seconds of fame will last a lifetime.

Sports embodies the spirit and embraces the soul. It provides moments that live within us for a lifetime. Sports brings people together; sports are not prejudiced, and even people who are have been known to leave that behind when faced with sports.

These are the things athletes represent – a dream that we all have had, the dream of excellence, facing and conquering challenges and fears. "Let me be great at something; God just give me one golden moment I can cherish for the rest of my life. Grace me with the spirit of a winner." Images of victories and failures like memories in time flash before our eyes. "If I could be great for one moment; let this be my time." The spotlight is on you for a few brief moments, and then it's gone. It brings a feeling of euphoria, and at times the illusion of immortality. Being the best: that's what it's all about – achieving the highest honor that only one person can achieve. A champion is the epitome of *success* who leaves everything else behind in a cloud of dust.

Memories of heroism are not tarnished by strikes; they outlive and endure generation after generation. Memories are handed down like heirlooms, sometimes from father to son or from mother to daughter. The spirit of victory will always remain in a champion's heart. Heroes who come through in the clutch, athletes that stand alone with the gold – that is what it is all about; reaching the highest echelon and raising your hands in victory.

Everyone I have ever known, whether they liked sports or disliked them, has always had a sports story, and a smile to go with it. This is true even if the story is about the non-athlete who played little league baseball, and 20 years later still remembers the ball that hit him in the head because he couldn't catch. That is representative of our culture. We root for the teams we rooted for all our lives – as if for moments in time, we can be the boy who listened to the World Series under his pillow on the radio, following Mickey Mantle and the Yankees or Roy Campanella and the Brooklyn Dodgers.

Associations with sports and sports celebrities spread images of trust, hard work, perseverance, skill, loyalty, style, and dependability in the public's eye.

New Sponsorship Signage Opportunities May Increase Revenue?

An overhead camera used during the Chicago Bulls telecasts has become a new advertising signage spot. Fletcher Chicago, the marketer of the camera, performed a research study and found that the distinctive shot generated strong awareness among TV viewers of the camera's sponsor, Upper Deck. Forty-three percent of the respondents in the study recognized Upper Deck's sponsor logo on the overhead camera.

Further research by the Chicago-based firm also revealed the effectiveness of traditional media of courtside advertising. Adtime signage showed a 47% recognition of at least one sponsor, and 61% named at least one in-game television sponsor. Reebok led Adtime signage recognition with 11%, followed by Gatorade, Nike, and Budweiser. However, Gatorade, Nike, and Budweiser's logos were not displayed on the Chicago Adtime's courtside. **1993 TRACY L. SCHOENADEL** *(SPORT INFORMATION SYSTEMS)*

Rotating courtside ads represent another form of advertising and team revenue-generating potential. In many cases, these ads may be more effective than 30-second commercial spots. Madison Square Garden is said to have raised nearly $100 million per season from its advertisers.

In the past couple of years, new products for increased advertising have been developed. Dorna, USA, which was formed in 1990, developed the "AdTime rotational signage system," to capture the interest of advertisers. In 1996-97, Dorna, USA sold out of advertising space for the NBA, which attracted $3 million in new sales. Dorna's system is sold to individual teams within leagues. The company's first league deal was with the American Basketball League. Currently, Dorna works with 19 NBA teams, 18 MLB teams, and 9 NHL Teams. **Staff. (1993, May). Broadcast news.** *Team Marketing Report,* **p.3.**

- **Rotating signage** and other forms of signage allow companies the ability to advertise during the actual contest, rather than in a commercial. The value of the rotating signs is calculated based upon the number of seconds a sponsor's ad is displayed. The sponsor's name or logo is clearly seen by a television spot during the event. The monetary value of this screen time is determined by comparing what the same amount of time would cost in the form of 30-second or one-minute commercials.

In the early 1990s, it was estimated that the sales value associated with the overall sports market, encompassing both participants and spectators, was more than $179 billion, with a steady increase of approximately 20% a year. Further indications that sports marketing is a fast-growing, multibillion-dollar business include the increasing number of promotions, corporate sponsorships and special events tied in with sporting events.

Between the years of 1981 and 1987, the number of promotion companies trying to supply the market for sports-oriented promotions increased from four to 400. In 1990 corporations spent

$23.52 billion in sports marketing. The 100 heaviest corporate spenders contributed only 9% of the total sports marketing expenditures (Advertising Age, 1991).

Advertising, licensing, promotional tie-ins, and sponsorships continue to increase as marketers look for new ways to reach consumers. Corporations realize they can reach consumers directly or indirectly through sports themes or tie-ins. Consumers have allegiance, loyalty, and dedication to teams.

In the modern era, ticket sales are no longer as important as the revenue brought in from product endorsements, merchandise licensing, and broadcast rights. Sponsorships of individual teams, leagues, and stadiums bring in millions of dollars in increased revenues. Simply put, sports is a business capitalizing on consumers.

Sports marketing in the past decade has grown to a billion-dollar global industry. Understanding your target market is essential when it comes to sports marketing. Leagues look at studies to find what market they are gaining and losing. This allows them to capture untapped age and occupational markets. Sports marketing has become as much a part of our culture as sports. But when is enough enough? Are people getting fed up with trying to figure out all the promotions, tie-ins, sponsors, etc.? The sports market is always fresh. Since public appearances by athletes began, team endorsements have gained popularity and creativity every year. Sports is a booming business, even when the economy is down. People will always attend sporting events and buy licensed merchandise.

Technology increases our access to sports information; talk radio, cable TV, and the Internet all shape the future of the information age. SportsLine USA brought all sports radio broadcasts to the World Wide Web. Still in the early stages of Internet, it appeared as if nothing was impossible – from radio broadcasts of your favorite teams to the eventual satellite feeds bringing TV broadcasts over the web. Future possibilities are amazing, and they are rapidly approaching with advanced technology leading the way.

People understand and are fascinated by sports and athletes. Sports marketing feeds on people's obsession for sports – we cannot get enough. This is especially true when players develop support in the community. However, we live in an imperfect world. Some athletes make headline news for negative reasons. What gets lost in all the negativity are the athletes who play with pride – who represent what is good in each of us and capture what it means to be an athlete. There are athletes who represent goodwill and good sportsmanship. There are athletes who play when they are injured for the good of the team, and there are athletes who give back to the community. Many athletes possess heart, but it seems at times we only hear, see, and read the negative aspects. This is when people ask the question, "What is wrong with sports?" In fact, the question should be, "What is right about sports?"

Sports marketing understands and tries to portray what the games represent. Upper Deck ran a commercial capturing the beauty and grace of Michael Jordan and Cal Ripken Jr. Throwback jerseys are popular, featuring legendary athletes like Dick Butkus, Roger Staubach, and Mean Joe Greene.

A Marketing Look at Baseball

Baseball, once known as the American "national pastime", has declined in popularity. It has been suggested that kids would rather dunk like Michael Jordan than hit a home run like Ken Griffey Jr. What has caused the decline? The strike of '94 hurt the game. The cancellation of the 1994 World Series due to a labor strike was hurtful to the game as well. These, however, are not necessarily the main reasons for the decline.

Baseball in America has a great history. It has offered the nation legends and larger-than-life heroes. For a long time, the Negro leagues were a part of American history that the public denied. The Negro leagues were the grassroots for men such as Jackie Robinson, Roy Campanella, and Ernie Banks. In recent years,

Negro league players have received the recognition they deserve. Men such as the ageless Satchel Paige and the speedy "Cool Papa" Bell, to name a few, have become Hall of Famers despite being segregated out of the major leagues. People still come out to meet men such as Buck O'Neil and the oldest living player, Ted "Double Duty" Radcliffe, who once caught for the legendary Satchel Paige.

Baseball may have begun to take the "national pastime" label for granted. The strike hurt the game as fans realized it had become little more than a business. Both the owners and the players appeared selfish.

Baseball, acknowledging a decline in fan support, formed a new marketing arm, Major League Baseball Enterprises. Gregory Murphy, the president and CEO of MLB Enterprises, said this about marketing the game: "Fans are feeling disenfranchised, that there's a level of anger, disappointment, and disgust out there that is notable and stunning." (*Baseball Business Journal*, July 1996). Can baseball re-market itself and regain the fans?

One of the areas and markets baseball has lost out on in the past decade or so is the inner cities. Kids see the game of basketball as a possible way out. High school kids are now applying for the NBA draft and passing up the chance to get a college education, which represents a confusion of values in our society. There are overwhelming odds against a prep athlete playing in the NFL or NBA, even with continuing expansion. People don't realize how few amateur and college athletes will ever make it professionally relative to the number who will try and fail.

The 1996 MLB All-Star Game may have illustrated the lack of interest people have for baseball. It received the lowest TV ratings for an All-Star game ever, since Neilsen ratings began in 1967. The low ratings indicate that it will take more marketing and time before people flock back to baseball. The 1996 All-Star ballots were sponsored by Texaco, and 10 million ballots were filled out – 4 million fewer than were filled out in 1994. The 1996 All-Star game may be a good example of how the fans feel about the game.

ALL STAR TV RATINGS 1967-1996

YEAR	NETWORK	RATING	SHARE	HH(000)
1967	NBC	25.6	50	14,050
1968	NBC	25.8	49	14,450
1969	NBC	15.1	42	8,610
1970	NBC	28.5	54	16,670
1971	NBC	27.0	50	16,230
1972	NBC	22.9	43	14,220
1973	NBC	23.8	45	15,420
1974	NBC	23.4	44	15,490
1975	NBC	21.5	41	14,730
1976	ABC	27.1	53	8,680
1977	NBC	24.5	45	17,440
1978	ABC	26.1	47	19,030
1979	NBC	24.4	45	18,180
1980	ABC	26.8	46	20,450
1981	NBC	20.1	36	15,640
1982	ABC	25.0	44	20,380
1983	NBC	21.5	39	17,910
1984	ABC	20.1	35	16,840
1985	NBC	20.5	36	17,400
1986	ABC	20.3	35	17,440
1987	NBC	18.2	37	15,910
1988	ABC	20.4	33	18,070
1989	NBC	18.2	33	16,450
1990	CBS	16.2	33	14,940
1991	CBS	17.4	32	16,200
1992	CBS	14.9	27	13,720
1993	CBS	15.6	28	14,550
1994	NBC	15.7	28	14,790
1995	ABC	13.9	25	13,260
1996	NBC	13.2	23	12,659

hh – households (thousands)   Source: Neilsen Media Research

However, the 1996 All-Star Fan Fest, an event held just before the All-Star Game, drew more than 103,000 visitors, the biggest ever attendance for a five-day Fan Fest.

The World Series Struck Out On TV

Neilson Media research reported that the Yankees' six-game victory over Atlanta received a 17.4 rating and a 29 share on Fox.

The rating – the percentage of television households watching the program – was the third lowest for any World Series, above only the earthquake-delayed series between Oakland and San Francisco in 1989 (16.4) and Toronto's victory over Philadelphia in 1993 (17.3).

The 1996 series' rating was 11% below the 19.5% for previous year's World Series between Atlanta and Cleveland.

Editor's Note: When baseball went up against football, it was a Monday night (Oct. 14, 1996). Baseball's prime spotlight included the NLCS between the Braves and the Cardinals. This prime-time match-up competed against Monday Night Football, a game between the Green Bay Packers and the San Francisco 49ers. In this head-to-head baseball and football comparison, football won by an astounding margin, amassing a Neilsen rating of 18.9, compared with the NLCS's rating of 7.0. Fox was the only network showing the 1996 World Series, between the Yankees and Braves. Game 2 was the lowest-rated World Series game ever in prime time, with a 14.0 rating and a 23 share. This game was on a Monday night. However, Monday Night Football, which is shown on ABC, earned a 12.2 rating, which incidentally was its lowest rating since 1986.

Ratings by game of the 1996 World Series aired on FOX (Rating/Share)			
Game 1	Sunday,	Oct 20	15.7/25
Game 2	Monday	Oct 21	14.0/23
Game 3	Tuesday	Oct 22	17.5/28
Game 4	Wednesday	Oct 23	17.9/32
Game 5	Thursday	Oct 24	20.0/32
Game 6	Saturday	Oct 26	19.1/34

The rating represents the number of households (in millions) watching the program. The share represents the percentage of all households with the television on at that time that were watching the World Series. (Associated Press New York – Even with the Yankees, the World Series had its lowest share of television viewers ever.)

Currently, baseball is hurting demographically. Baseball appeals to people aged 50 years and older. People in the ages 40-50 are more interested in football. Basketball is the choice sport for people 24-

40. Hockey appeals to fans 24 and under. For baseball, these demographics are not good. The sport's main target will be collecting social security soon. The baby boomers – currently the largest market – are not as interested in baseball anymore. The strike did the most damage. People were outraged, feeling that the game had let them down, and as a result they protested by staying away. Baseball must work to restore the damage. The fans viewed the players as being selfish and greedy, when in fact it was both the players and the owners. That doesn't really matter. The fact is that the 1994 World Series never happened.

The positive side of baseball was the postseason of 1995. The playoffs included the excitement of watching Ken Griffey Jr.'s heroics vs. the Yankees, when the underdog Seattle Mariners team pulled off the upset. The upshot Cleveland Indians had a remarkable season, only to fall short to the Atlanta Braves in the World Series. The game's top pitcher, Greg Maddux, won an unprecedented fourth consecutive Cy Young Award. Albert Belle was the first player in baseball history to have over 50 home runs and 50 doubles in the same season, achieving this during a strike-shortened year consisting of 143 games instead of 162. Another bright spot for baseball in 1995 was Cal Ripken Jr.'s pursuit of "The Streak." Ripken broke Lou "Iron Horse" Gehrig's consecutive games played streak of 2,130. Television ratings were high, and so was the beauty of baseball as Ripken took his jog around the Camden Yards infield, a moment that transcended the image of what baseball has become.

A comparative study done in April revealed the following information:

Game attendance averages/major leagues			
April 1995 vs. April 1996			
(Data supplied by Baseball Weekly)			
	April 1995	April 1996	Pct. Change
American League avg.	23,306	25,423	Plus 9.1%
National League avg.	24,658	25,285	Plus 2.5%
Composite AL and NL	47,964	50.708	Plus 5.7%
Avg. Attendance	23,982	25,354	Plus 5.7%

The increase did not last long. The average attendance in 1994 was 31,612, and the 1996 average was 26,338 – a negative difference of 5,274 per game. In the league as a whole, that was a drop of nearly 80,000 fans in attendance a night.

In an effort to restore fans, the Major League Baseball Players Association has introduced a new brand of merchandise – MLB Players' Choice. Licensed items will be promoted by the slogan, "It's Outta Here." The items will be targeted toward children between the ages of 8 and 14 (and their parents). Baseball is finally realizing that children are the future of the game. Demographically, women – specifically mothers between ages 30 and 45 – listed baseball as their favorite sport, but the majority looked at baseball as a social event.

The strike did not hurt the minor leagues. In fact, the minor leagues secured some benefits from the problems of MLB. People still love the game of baseball and its storied heroes such as Mantle and Dimaggio, Ted Williams, and Duke Snider. Today's players simply do not have the mystique possessed by the heroes of yesterday. The minor leagues have a unique following of people in a community. Fans get the chance to see some of the minor league players that may one day make it to the major leagues. The growth of the minor leagues will impact baseball positively, mostly due to the more affordable ticket prices and the teams' creative promotions. Minor League Baseball attendance has been healthy and strong, and was up in 1996.

Minor league attendance the last five years:	
Year	Attendance
1992	27,180,170
1993	30,022,761
1994	33,355,199
(The year Major League Baseball was on strike)	
1995	33,126,934
1996	33,289,278
Source: NAPBL	

The route baseball will take to restore its fan base is to promote the game itself – a strategy that may be difficult, because many people are convinced that "baseball is boring." The logical step for MLB's marketing plan will be to promote the new heroes of the game – Frank Thomas, Barry Bonds, Greg Maddux, Ken Griffey Jr., etc. However, it will take more than promotions of stars to get fans to come back to the game. There isn't one particular thing baseball needs to do to recapture its fans. It will take time and marketing. Promoting heroes always seems like the most accessible method of rejuvenating the game; the pursuit of records always seems to excite people. The most untouchable record – but arguably the most prestigious – is home runs in a season. This record is held by Roger Maris, who hit 61 home runs in 1961. Every year, if a player starts off hot, everyone seem to want to follow the excitement and the pursuit of records. 1996, of course, was a year in which the ball was wound so tight that tremendous numbers of runs were scored, threatening offensive records and attracting people to watch the games – just a theory. In the '70s, there were people calling a curveball an optical illusion.

Baseball is serious about marketing itself – serious enough to begin Major League Baseball Enterprises. MLB Enterprises was specifically designed to market the game and to find ways for baseball to recapture the public's trust. Acting commissioner Bud Selig said this about MLB Enterprises:

"Major League Baseball Enterprises represents a bold attempt by Major League Baseball to strategically integrate its revenue-producing entities for optimum growth. The formation of Major League Baseball Enterprises will be vital to the game's success as we move into the 21st century."

Gregory Murphy was named president and CEO of the new venture. Murphy has a serious marketing background and an impressive resume. He was president and CEO of Kraft Foods Bakery Companies from 1987 to 1995. In 1987, Kraft Foods Bakery had a total revenue base of $650 million. In 1995, total revenue was $1.5 billion under Murphy's leadership. Baseball realizes the importance of immediate steps, and this is a first step in the right direction.

Murphy said, "Major League Baseball possesses great potential to be a business leader, not only in the sports marketplace, but in a vast international marketplace that includes a myriad of entertainment and product choices. As a life-long baseball fan and career marketing professional, I am looking forward to the challenge of developing strategies that will increase revenue, increase attendance, increase television ratings, and increase franchise values, and make Major League Baseball an international sports and entertainment leader."

Baseball still has its work cut out for it. The group baseball is losing is teenagers – the 12-17 age group – and males 18-34. In trying to recapture teenagers, the league should be restoring fields and sparking interest in the inner cities and their surrounding communities.

Baseball will survive the negative response it has received of late. In 1996, home runs provided an exciting lift to the game, and runs were scored in droves. Time will slowly run its course, and the October Classic is always electric. Toward the end of the 1996 baseball season, attendance began to pick up. This increase may have been made possible by the recent addition of wild-card teams to the playoff structure. More cities were given the opportunity to attain a place in the postseason. The playoffs are heavily watched, and the wild-card addition should increase the excitement and length of pennant races and get fans back to the ballpark. The addition of wild-card teams has been positive. Baseball's postseason has been a great part of our October culture, and now more cities can share in this experience.

Baseball also split the broadcasts of 1996 postseason games between NBC, Fox Sports, ESPN, and ESPN2. Major League Baseball attracted more viewers, and every postseason game was broadcast nationwide. In addition, Major League Baseball International produced a live worldwide television feed to televise both League Championship Series. The World Series was then distributed to 200 countries and was broadcast live in five different languages. It was distributed by six different rights holders: NHK Japan in Japanese; Televisa and Prime Deportiva in Spanish; TVIS Taiwan in Mandarin, and Supersport Benelux in Dutch. Baseball is expanding, and the success of prominent Latin superstars around the league helps in the Spanish market.

Final 1996 Baseball Attendance Figures

The mid-season attendance figures made it seem as if baseball could never be restored, but a second look at baseball attendance figures offers great hope that the league can win back baseball fans and introduce more to the sport. Though MLB began the 1996 season in a slump, by the end of the year baseball attendance had topped 60 million. This was only the second time in baseball history that attendance was over 60 million. The second-highest total attendance of 60,096,451 was surpassed only by 70,256,459 in 1993. The average attendance for games in 1996 was 26,889 – the fifth most in league history. Every major league team exceeded one million in total home attendance, and overall attendance increased 6.1% over figures from 1995. In 1994 the average fan attendance for a game was 31,612 (before the strike). Four teams were over three million (Los Angeles Dodgers, Cleveland Indians, Baltimore Orioles, and Colorado Rockies).

Cal Ripken's quest to break the record for playing the most consecutive baseball games has made him one of the most sought-after spokesmen in marketing. Ripken was at one point considering a dozen national endorsements with more than 100 licensing proposals, and countless offers from the collectibles market – all of which can be the basis of tie-ins for sports promotions and incentives. However, when Ripken broke the world record in Kansas City, the Royals drew a little over 20,000 fans – 50% of their stadium's capacity.

For baseball to be restored fully, MLB may have to take a page out of the NBA marketing program from the early '80s – the early years of Magic Johnson and Larry Bird, two marquee stars who paved the way for current players. Basketball may be the strongest worldwide sport next to soccer. The marketing of basketball usually resembles that of a heavyweight title boxing match: Shaquille O'Neal vs. Hakeem Olajuwon, Michael Jordan vs. Clyde Drexler. Although it is a team game, basketball as a marketing concept revolves around the superstars of the game. Baseball doesn't seem to replicate the aura basketball sometimes possesses, as if it were a two-man match-up. Baseball is marketed more toward corporate sponsorship, and is losing touch with the fans.

Until recently, American football has been limited on a worldwide basis, compared to soccer, baseball, and basketball. However, the World League of professional football was formed, and it became a minor league for NFL franchises, giving young players the opportunity to develop and get some seasoning. Teams were distributed globally, with locations including: Amsterdam; Barcelona, Spain; Frankfurt, Germany; London, England; Dusseldorf, Germany; and Scotland. This was a good introduction to the American version of football for European markets. This exposure became an important aspect of the game, allowing the NFL to introduce and capture markets outside the USA. NFL sponsored the Punt, Pass, and Kick competition, which in 1995 allowed 400,000 kids to participate across the world.

Expansion plays a large role in marketing. The NFL currently plays preseason games in Tokyo and Mexico. These exhibition games are marketing tools paving the way for new markets outside the United States. The bottom line is that more merchandise equals more money for football.

Commissioner Paul Tagliabue has told the media he is committed to the Japanese market. American football has been played in Japan since 1934. In 1989 the NFL began playing what was called the "American Bowl" in Tokyo during the preseason. In the late 1996, the NFL teamed up with two Japanese companies – Bunka Hoso Brain and Detsu Corporation – in an effort to increase interest in American football in Japan. NFL JapanLink will continue this effort, distributing information to Japan using the media, promotions, and supporting NFL fan clubs.

The NFL teamed up with Coca-Cola in 1996 to a tune of $20 million, the largest ever promotion by the NFL. This effort began in movie theaters, with the joint Coca-Cola and NFL Films promotion "The Coca-Cola/NFL Red Zone Watch And Win." The promotion gives viewers a chance to win Super Bowl tickets. The "Red Zone" is everywhere that Coca-Cola products are available. The effort looked to capitalize on the excitement of football and to promote NFL-licensed products.

National Football League International was formed to assist the league in marketing the NFL worldwide. Strategically, the NFL is aware of the popularity of American football throughout the world. This will boost sales of NFL licensed merchandise and league promotion. NFL International will focus on international operations, which will include merchandising, sponsorship, television distribution, and licensing.

In the 1996-97 National Hockey League season, the NHL looked to capitalize on its growing popularity in the United States with the slogan "Coolest Game on Earth." The NHL is hoping to capture an 18-34 age demographic fan base while marketing to become the fourth most popular sport in North America. The NHL has looked to gain momentum, attracting corporate sponsors such as

Anheuser-Busch, Campbell Soup Company, Sears & Roebuck, and Quaker State Company. Hockey is looking to capitalize upon its increasing popularity by running a $10 million image campaign. Conflicting with this image campaign is a promotional campaign of the Pittsburgh Penguins and Arby's, a restaurant chain that sponsors the team. The "Arby's Beef of the Game" promotion refers to – and indirectly encourages – on-ice fights. The NHL will also work on the "NHL Freeze Play" – a six-week hockey tutorial held at various rinks in the Philadelphia and Toronto markets. Next season, the league will look to expand this program to reach all 26 markets with NHL teams.

Soccer's popularity has grown steadily in the United States. The 1994 World Cup was so positive and exciting that ABC finished with a 9.5 rating for the title game and an 11-game average rating of 5.3 (five million households), well above expectations. The extensive coverage gave viewers a more in-depth look at the personality of the game. Soccer, taking a page out of NBA promotions, plans to market individual players in the future.

AC Milan superstar George Weah signed on with Edge Sports International to market himself as a superstar. Currently, soccer lacks the individual superstars other sports promote. Weah is considered to be the best player in the world, and he is currently under contract with Diadoara. Weah could be a great boost for soccer in America. He is currently under a three-year contract, but once the contract expires in 1999, the African native may play in America's Major League Soccer. If the marketing of this international star is successful in the United States, it would be great for the game and promotion of soccer.

Basketball has been a global sport for quite some time, and although we don't think of the Harlem Globetrotters as a professional basketball team, they may have been the first team to introduce basketball to other countries – the original ambassadors to the world for the sport. The Globetrotters have been promoting basketball worldwide for over 70 years. In 1951, the Globetrotters played in Berlin's Olympic Stadium to a crowd of 75,000, the largest crowd ever assembled to watch a basketball game. The Globetrotters may not get the credit they deserve globally, but they always put on a good show. In the modern era of basketball, the Globetrotters should be acknowledged for their contribution to the game. We should not forget what they have done for basketball globally by performing in public arenas and always eliciting smiles from children and adults. The Harlem Globetrotters currently have two travel teams and continue their global play.

NBA basketball has a certain style and showmanship. Guys like Dennis Rodman, Michael Jordan, and Shaquille O'Neal can at any given moment take over a game. There is a greater sense of entertainment about basketball, which is why baseball and other sports cannot market the same way. In 1995, the "Sporting News

Top 100 Most Powerful" people in sports listed Michael Jordan #44 and Shaquille O'Neal #50.

The NBA has without a doubt been the league that has benefited the most from marketing. During the 1980-81 season, 16 of the 23 teams lost money. The average attendance was 58% capacity for each game. The average player salary was $325,000. Television ratings were low, and domestic licensing revenue was less than $10 million. David Stern was then named NBA commissioner. Many consider the entrance of both Larry Bird – drafted by the Boston Celtics out of Indiana State – and Ervin "Magic" Johnson – drafted by the Los Angeles Lakers out of Michigan State – to be turning points for basketball's marketability. The two players faced off against each other in the NCAA basketball championship, in which Michigan State prevailed. Without strategic marketing by the NBA, the success of individuals could not have made the league profitable.

David Stern turned the ailing league into a billion-dollar global marketing success story. He played a major role in creating NBA Properties, the marketing arm of the NBA. He modeled the organization after National Football League's NFL Properties.

David Stern, along with Rick Welts, current president of NBA Properties, took sports marketing to a new level. Gross retail sales of logos and NBA player likenesses are nearly $3 billion a year.

Current attendance figures average nearly 90% of stadium capacity. The NBA received a television contract worth over $1.1 billion over four years. Player salaries now average over a million dollars a year.

The Big Money

Michael Jordan	$30,140,000	Chicago
Horace Grant	$17,857,142	Orlando
Shaquille O'Neal	$10,714,286	L.A. Lakers
Gary Payton	$10,211,880	Seattle
David Robinson	$9,952,070	San Antonio
Hakeem Olajuwon	$9,655,000	Houston
Alonzo Mourning	$9,379,800	Miami
Juwan Howard	$9,375,000	Washington
Dennis Rodman	$9,000,000	Chicago
Dikembe Mutombo	$8,012,656	Atlanta
Chris Webber	$8,000,000	Washington
Otis Thorpe	$7,000,000	Detroit
Latrell Sprewell	$7,000,000	Golden State
Elden Campbell	$7,000,000	L.A. Lakers
Kevin Johnson	$7,000,000	Phoenix
Danny Manning	$6,833,333	Phoenix
Derrick Coleman	$6,739,200	Philadelphia
Anfernee Hardaway	$6,655,000	Orlando
Dale Davis	$6,508,333	Indiana
Clyde Drexler	$5,500,000	Houston

The average NBA salary increased by between 13% and 16% in each of the past three seasons. This year, though, the average salary will jump about 27%. (Reprinted with permission from the Newark, N.J., *Star Ledger*.)

Average NBA salary in millions

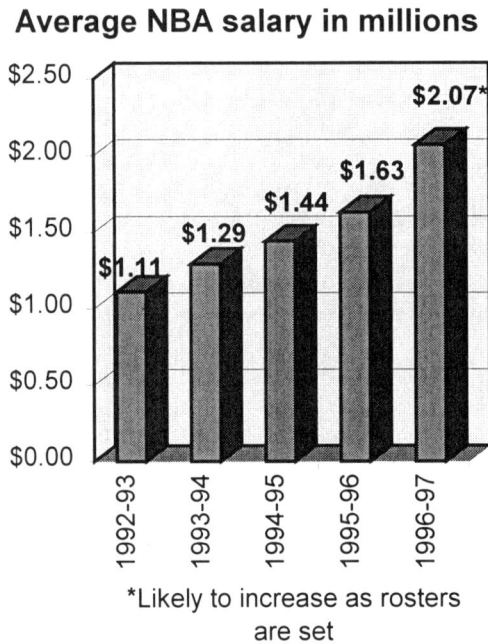

*Likely to increase as rosters are set

NBA Properties and the league evaluate team logos, uniform colors, and team uniforms. This is an effort to stimulate the retail sales market and the demand for NBA-licensed merchandise. In 1996, teams added a third uniform to their rotation of home and away uniforms.

The NBA is also sensitive to issues facing society. It was announced that the Washington Bullets would be changed to the Washington Wizards in an effort to promote a less violent image than what was associated with the word "bullets." NBA Properties is responsible for the new team logo, colors, and uniforms.

From a national and international standpoint, NBA basketball is rapidly becoming the world's favorite game. For example, look at some of the NBA players who have come into the league from other countries: Sarunas Marciulionis, Toni Kukoc, Vlade Divac, Luc Longely, Hakeem Olujuwan, Dino Radja, Gheorge Muhresan, Manute Bol, and Dikembe Mutombo, to name a few.

The 1996 world champion Chicago Bulls may have given us a glimpse of the future. It was a team that featured Luc Longely (Australia) and Toni Kukoc (Croatia), Michael Jordan (USA), and others. In the future, the NBA may become increasingly international, with several countries represented on each team. This will promote NBA basketball globally.

Chapter 2

Marketing Products Through Sports

One of the most important aspects of marketing through sports is locating a target market for the product.

The following information was compiled by The Taylor Group, Inc. It comes from a national survey commissioned by NBA Properties Inc. and based on 1,033 respondents, ages 8 to 17. Information was collected by a phone survey from 3/30/96 to 4/22/96 (percentages not available).

Sport Preferences - Ages 8 to 17

Ages 8 - 11	Ages 12-17
Rank	Rank
1. NBA	1. NBA Basketball
2. NFL	2. NFL Football
3. MLB	3. MLB Baseball
4. Soccer	4. Soccer
5. NHL	5. NHL Hockey
6. NCAA Basketball	6. Auto Racing
7. NCAA Football	7. NCAA Basketball
8. Auto Racing	8. NCAA Football

Top 11 Most Popular U.S. Sports - All Ages

12,018 respondents – 12-month phone survey - 4/1/95 to 3/31/95
Data Supplied by Sponsorship Research International

Rank &Sport	Pct.
1. Olympics	69%
2. NFL Football	64
3. (tie) Major League Baseball	50
4. (tie) College Football	50
5. NBA Basketball	47
6. College Basketball	42
7. (tie) NASCAR Racing	32
8. (tie) Indy Car Racing	32
9. NHL Hockey	26
10. NHRA Drag Racing	23
11. Soccer	18

Relationship Marketing

Companies are now studying the concept of *relationship marketing*. This approach views spectators as consumers. Studies using this approach focus on finding the motives factoring into marketing success, looking at the relationship of product sales and attendance at sports events. The purpose is to find conclusive evidence measuring fan loyalty by viewing spectators as consumers. The concept of relationship marketing gives insight into what sells by utilizing fan attendance.

Event/ Sport	Facility Type	Length of Stay (hrs.)
Pro football	Stadium	6
College football	Stadium	5
Major League Baseball	Stadium	6
Minor league baseball	Stadium	6
Motorcross	Stadium	5
Rock concert	Stadium	6
Rock concert	Arena	4
NBA basketball	Arena	3
Pro soccer	Stadium	4
Ice hockey	Arena	3
Boxing	Arena	3
Horse race	Horse track	4
Auto race	Auto track	4

There are also new sports markets that can be entered into for endorsement and marketing purposes. Arena football is selling out in Phoenix, Ariz., and Orlando, Fla., in its 10th season. First-year franchises in San Jose, Calif., and Memphis, Tenn., drew averages of 6,000 and 5,000 fans, respectively, per game this past season. When marketing to arena football fans, it is important to know the typical fan is a professional male between the ages of 30-36, who generally can't afford seats to NFL games, or whose employer offers tickets to the worst match-ups. Top deck seats at arena football games sell for $10, luxury seats for $79.50, and season tickets for $175. The average per capita spending on food and beverages is $5.30, with Orlando posting the high of $7.50. All these statistics on fans and their spending habits help to determine how to market for these spectators/consumers, and who should do the marketing. During the years of major sports league strikes, this type of affordable entertainment gains visibility because of its affordability.

Children are not the only ones wearing sports teams' logos. The person who wore his favorite team's baseball cap as a child probably is still wearing it, maybe with the new logo on it. Actually, clothing featuring a sports team is more often purchased for an adult (55%) rather than for a child (33%). These figures were compiled through a Sports Services of America™ phone survey in which 150 people were polled – 82 females and 68 males.

In a recent survey it was found that 60% of households polled had some items with a sports team logo on it. Of the 200 people surveyed, 115 were males and 85 were females, and respondents fell between the ages of 17 and 55. This 60% is broken-down as follows between different types of merchandise:

T-shirts	17%
Baseball caps	10%
Golf shirts	9%
Sweatshirts	9%

In the same survey, these are the sports with the largest share of the sports merchandise market.

Football	40%
Basketball	32%
Baseball	16%
Hockey	5%
Car racing	4%

Sports teams add meaning and value to products by communicating allegiance. Of those surveyed, 39% said they felt like a real fan and felt supportive when wearing merchandise with their team's logo. This allegiance can be harnessed into merchandise sales. Popular sports teams inspire a growing business of specialty entertainment retail licensing.

One of the more effective methods of marketing is to link the attributes of the athlete with the attributes of a product. For example, in a recent car ad campaign, the company linked the moves of Barry Sanders to the precision handling of its car. A pair of Nike "Air Jordans" can improve your jumping ability; you will be able to defy gravity just as Jordan does. If you drink Gatorade, you can play like Jordan. Using athlete attributes in marketing has proven to be successful in selling products.

Gross Impression

What I call "sports gross impression" is the number of impressions made associating a product or service with an athlete, team, or sport. Exposure to a product – whether it's by sound, sight or smell – often causes an effect on consumers. The message is subliminally planted in the mind of the consumer. The *gross impression* is the bottom line in advertising and a way of gaining publicity through sports. An excellent example was the 1996 Olympic Summer Games. How many times did you see an athlete with a Nike "swoosh" on his or her apparel?

Any time you go to a basketball game and see the Nike "swoosh" or Reebok symbol, that is a gross impression. You may not look at the shoe as making an impression, but it does. There is an enormous amount of money being spent on college and professional teams' apparel, and logos are now being put directly on the uniforms. In the past, this was unheard of. Penn State uniforms feature the Nike "swoosh" on their jerseys. This makes a very big impression – an impression traditional paid advertising does not make. People want to be associated with elite teams and athletes. Gross impression represents this association.

Controversial Dennis Rodman, while promoting his book *Bad As I Wanna Be*, dressed in drag – silver nails, red wig, scarf, and hat. Through self-promotion, Rodman created a situation in which it was not necessary to advertise the book through the usual outlets. He had become one of the most recognizable athletes, constantly in the spotlight on television, radio, magazines, and newspapers across America. Once again, an example of gross impression – the number of media mentions. His visibility and hair colors make an unavoidable impression. Over 10,000 fans lined up to see "The Worm" at a book signing. Did the relationship between the athlete and the book fit together? Absolutely; it was a great example of self promotion, resulting in over 650,000 copies sold in one week – that's $13 million dollars in gross receipts sold. GRO$$ Impression.

During the 1995-96 season, the Chicago Bulls had the most wins by a team in one season in NBA history (72). Michael Jordan picked up his fourth MVP trophy, along with an MVP in the NBA Finals. The season captured the attention not only of sports fans, but of non-sports fans as well. Michael Jordan was back on the endorsement circuit, as were Dennis Rodman and Scottie Pippen. The affiliation of a champion is enticing to the fan. Chicago Bulls merchandise sold out of stores as quickly as it came in. Dennis

Rodman, Scottie Pippen, and Michael Jordan all had shoe contracts with the same company. The more visible the athlete or team, the more fans associate the athletes with the product. This association is the trademark of gross impression.

The Battle Rages On

Thirty years ago, Philip Knight formed a company to import high-quality running shoes to the U.S. The company was eventually named Nike, after the Greek goddess of victory. By the time Nike went public in 1980, revenues had reached $270 million. The first year Nike signed Michael Jordan, the company named a line of merchandise "Air Jordans." The line of footwear and apparel was a flashy collection in black and red, and it brought in over $100 million in new revenue. Reebok and Nike control over 40% of the global market.

The competition between Nike and Reebok heated up as the 1996 Summer Games approached. The shoe giants competed for Olympic advertising and Olympic athlete endorsements in their efforts to dominate the athletic shoe industry. At stake in this fierce battle between Nike and Reebok over athletic shoes is a $13 billion-a-year business in the United States alone, and there are growing markets for other sports apparel as well. Who will wear Nike? Who will wear Reebok? Fans have come to enjoy the corporate rivalries, as well as the creative advertising, marketing, and promotional ploys designed in the spirit of competition.

Ambush Marketing

Stealth mark [handwritten annotation]

Once the 1996 Olympic Games began, Reebok had a TV edge. It purchased exclusive rights to advertise athletic footwear on NBC Olympic broadcasts. However, Nike had purchased air time on local radio stations and competing networks. Nike also strategically placed several billboards around the Atlanta area. These are practices that fall in the category of stealth or ambush marketing.

During the 1992 Olympics, Reebok was the official sponsor. Nike used its endorsed athletes for commercials. Olympic exposure and ad time made it look as if Nike was the official Olympic sponsor. The ads painted the athletes' desire to win: the grueling faces of weary athletes striving with all their heart and soul to win. These types of commercials fall into the stealth category. A company can advertise using Olympic athletes without being an official sponsor, and these stealth campaigns drove the official sponsors crazy, which was the purpose. There is no sure-fire way to stop stealth marketing, but the Olympic Committee tries to monitor it.

Nike designed a track suit with "swooshes" instead of stars on the American flag. By Olympic commercialization standards, that design violated rules limiting logo count.

Simply put, "ambush marketing" and "stealth marketing" refer to sponsor organizations participating in events rather than sponsoring the events. Reebok was not an Olympic Sponsor when the games were in Lillihammer in '94, but Reebok's visibility was high because it sponsored the Russian Olympic Committee and the International Ice Hockey Federation. Reebok's marquee spokesperson at the time was Nancy Kerrigan.

Was This Strategy Successful?

Absolutely! Twenty-four percent of those polled after the 1994 Lillihammer games thought Reebok was an official Olympic sponsor. Although 24% may seem to be a small percentage, it's significant because it could have increased Reebok sales. People tend to relate brands to sports – that alone can influence someone to buy Reebok, as opposed to another brand.

Currently, what makes the market so competitive is the struggle over putting logos on the uniforms of professional and college sports teams. The interesting thing about this competition is that 10 years ago, these manufacturers were not vying to have logos on uniforms. Now at the college and pro level, these companies battle for market share and exposure.

The buzz around Barcelona was that Jordan, Barkley, and other Nike-endorsed members of the 1992 U.S. Olympic basketball team were not happy. The problem was that Reebok had paid for the privilege of designing the warm-up suits to be used at the gold-medal ceremony. When the big moment came, Jordan, Barkley, and the other Nike-endorsed athletes draped American flags over their shoulders and rolled back their collars to obscure the Reebok logo.

Nike was not an official 1996 Olympic sponsor, but if you looked at the athletes, it was be hard not to notice the number of them wearing Nike apparel with the "swoosh" trademark. These high-profile athletes graced the covers of magazines ranging from *Sports Illustrated* to *Ad Age*. The Nike "swoosh" was so prominent that it is difficult to determine who exactly was the Olympic clothing sponsor. It was Reebok.

Currently, manufacturers such as Nike, Reebok, Wilson, Converse, and Champion go after professional teams for uniform logo visibility. This illustrates the direction in which athletic shoe manufacturers are going in their efforts to gain market share. The day may come when a Reebok athlete plays for a Nike-supported team and wants to get a Reebok uniform logo to match his teammates who are wearing the Nike swoosh. The market may dictate behaviors of the individuals instead of the concept of the team. Emmitt Smith, Dallas Cowboy running back, is endorsed by Reebok, while the Cowboys are endorsed by Nike. The day may come when Smith will have a Dallas Cowboy uniform with a Reebok logo.

In 1969, the NFL sold $19 million in licensed products. In 1986, the NFL almost tripled that total, with retail sales estimated at nearly $1 billion. NFL Properties has approximately 400 licensees manufacturing about 4,000 products.

There are many different types of license agreements. A group license agreement encompasses all members of that particular group. For example, an NFL team license grants the rights to use all the NFL team logos; while one must get a Players' Association license if one wishes to use an individual athlete's name or likeness on a product. It gets even more complicated. If you want a quarterback, such as Dan Marino or other high-profile NFL players, a separate license is required from "The Quarterback Club."

Every licenser grants certain regional or limited licenses, usually for one particular entity in a specific area. All licenses are negotiable. Generally, a royalty rate based on a percentage of sales and a guarantee is required – a 5-10% royalty on the wholesale price of the item. Licenses are generally good for two years. A guaranteed amount is usually required. For example, $20,000 for insurance may be required on items, a requirement of traditional retail sales only. When using athletes or teams in an appearance, remember that certain rules may apply, such as that if one uses four or more current players for a promotion, a license from the Players' Association may be required. If an athlete is retired and is not a member of an association, a license may not be required. Even though an athlete may not be a member of an association (not paying dues), he may still be a part of the association, depending on the league.

A complete outline of a product includes product samples, an artist's drawing, an advertising plan, a price breakdown, and existing distribution networks. When sending a sample product to a league or institution, it is not generally required that the league's logo be on the product.

Chapter 3

Sponsorship

What is Sponsorship?

Sponsorship is when a company, organization, or individual pays money or donates products and services for recognition. Leagues, athletes, teams, and stadiums can all be sponsored.

Soccer has been going through steady growth in the United States. Soccer, along with tennis, is among the few sports that allow sponsors to print their company names on competitive apparel. Sponsoring companies usually place a sponsor patch on the shirt, headband, wristband, shoes, or socks. During Major League Soccer's first year in existence, it received $50 million dollars in sponsor commitments. Individuals can be sponsored without having a team sponsorship. Soccer player Alexi Lalas is sponsored by Naya Water, and tennis player Andre Agassi is sponsored by Nike. The sponsorship of team sports is heading in the direction of sponsored advertisements. Organizations like Nike, Wilson, Champion, and Reebok bid to sponsor teams. The significant thing is the logo on the uniform, and sponsored patches usually do not have any advantage over simple logos. Although soccer and tennis are two sports that allow visible sponsor patches, the company logos on the uniforms serve the same purpose.

Auto racing has been measured to be the number-one sport for fan loyalty (*examples are shown later in this chapter*). This indicates that auto racing fans are also the most loyal to the sponsors of their favorite drivers or teams. Sponsors are able to get recognition with their logos on the driver's uniform, helmet, and car. Sponsors receive great visibility from the fans at the event and the fans who watch the event on television. Sponsors may receive additional publicity if the company name is mentioned during the broadcast, and they may receive added exposure if their sponsored team or driver is victorious.

While sports marketing has existed for a long period of time, it is common now for the word "niche" marketing to be used. Companies do extensive research to find niches and to measure sponsorship value packages based on targeted markets. Every sponsored event has a package of benefits accompanied by a proposal. In the proposal, there is a demographic breakdown of those who attend the event. Some of the more common niche markets include women, seniors, "Generation X-ers," and various ethnic groups. Sponsors try to appeal to consumers from these diversified markets, and at the same time to introduce their products to targeted new markets.

Sponsorship is not limited to any particular sport. Large companies such as Anheuser-Busch increase their sponsorship portfolio by moving into "lifestyle" sports, which include volleyball, jet skiing, and snowboarding. Many companies sponsor lifestyle sports mainly because of their relatively low cost and their demographic market. The ESPN X-Games are extreme sports, and as X-Games increase in popularity, exposure of sponsorships also increases. Companies can afford to sponsor smaller events and benefit from the recognition, signage, and publicity. It comes down to cost-efficiency and exposure. Companies should be aware of the target market for each event they sponsor, spending less on second-tier events and getting more of a value for their money. The X-Games are an example of an affordable yet increasingly popular sports program with which to advertise.

Sponsoring the X-Games is a great way to reach the demographic population in the tough-to-market 13-24 age group. The average on-site age was 20, and 66% of the attendees were under the age of 21. The primary audience was male (70%).

Ninety percent of attendees described the X-Games as "the wave of the future," while 91% said it is "a good reflection of today's youth." Ninety-seven percent said it is "not boring," while 24% felt that it was "over-commercialized" and 28% said it was "too limited."

Although respondents were aided in questioning regarding corporate sponsors, 92% were generally aware of Mountain Dew, 85% of Taco Bell, 80% of Nike, and 75% of Coors Light as sponsors. Sponsors not recognized were AT&T by 62% and Chevy Trucks by 55%.

32% of attendees reported that they would "almost always" or "frequently" select an X-Game sponsor's product over a non-sponsor's product.

In total, 311 respondents were interviewed for this study at the various locations. Testing was conducted on-site during the games, June 24-30, 1996. The margin of error for this study is no more than $\pm$ 5%.

Marketing directors have latched onto sponsorship in a big way in recent years, but it is not a blind infatuation. Pressure on budgets force clients to be responsible and sophisticated about their sponsorship dollars. Companies need reassurance that their investments are working, and they have turned to market research to deliver, measuring the results of their sponsorship. Through the purchase of advertising space and sponsorship, a client buys a guaranteed amount of exposure. That exposure must be profitable, or the campaign is pulled from the airwaves and the sponsorship is altered.

In the current world of sports, anything can be sponsored and everything is fair game. There is even opportunity to sponsor Cowboy owner Jerry Jones's radio show on KLIF in Dallas on Tuesdays for $72,750. There are slots for two non-competing sponsors for a cost of $72,750. Here is what you receive: one weekly 60-second ad during the show (there are 19 total shows), opening and closing billboards, and 256 60-second ads throughout the season. The show runs from August to December. There are more perks, but that at least gives an idea of what the sponsorship entails – the chance to cash in on Jerry Jones' popularity.

Controversies surrounding sponsorship have prevented certain types of companies from sponsoring sporting events. Alcohol, cigarette, and tobacco companies are targeted. In baseball, the

Atlanta Braves made it to the postseason in 1996. Phillip Morris removed its billboard from Atlanta-Fulton County Stadium, where the Braves play. This came with an agreement from the United States Justice Department. The Marlboro cigarette billboard was located on the outfield wall. Phillip Morris still had nine bulletin boards throughout the stadium, but these were out of the view of television cameras. However, in Yankee Stadium, the Marlboro billboard remained in view for everyone to see.

The Justice Department is working to eliminate alcohol, cigarette, and tobacco advertisements from stadiums and professional sports by the end of 1997. This effort includes NASCAR, in which cigarette and tobacco companies spend millions of dollars on sponsorship.

How Does One Find a Sponsor?

Sponsorship of smaller community events and secondary sports is growing. The reason for this growth is that companies look for sponsored events to gain recognition. One must understand the target market of the event and know the demographics. Who does your event reach? What gender? What age group? What income ranges? Once you have ascertained the demographic make-up of the event, the next task is to contact organizations that could potentially benefit. It is essential to research companies you approach. Knowledge is power. Find out what they have sponsored in the past. What are they sponsoring now? Know who their target market is. You want to create a win/win presentation. What do they get for their sponsorship? What package are you offering? What type of marketing will be done to promote the sponsored event? What can you do for them? Find out how much marketing they are willing to do. Sponsors don't benefit without doing their own marketing or promotion. *(See Chapter 4 for samples of full sponsorship proposals.)*

Make corporate and business contacts in your area. Be persistent and polished during all correspondence, whether it be by phone or in person. Have a brochure ready to send if a contact is interested, and mail it right away. Make sure to follow up with a telephone call.

Corporations Want Viability and Effectiveness

- Increase product or company awareness, including name recognition.

- Shape the awareness of the company, product, or service so it ties in with a particular lifestyle.

- Enhance a firm's community profile and commitment to the community.

- Improve corporate identity.

- Generate goodwill by associating with sports.

Is Sponsorship Effective? It Depends

Measuring sponsorship is a hot topic in sports. Take into consideration the John Hancock Bowl, which was held in El Paso, Texas, and sponsored by John Hancock Financial Services. In 1987, it was estimated that a $1.6 million event sponsorship generated $5.1 million of advertising exposure. This was not an easy task. The year prior to the bowl game, John Hancock scoured magazines and newspapers across the country, counting the number of stories about its bowl, and generating numbers on column inches, circulation, and ad rates. They also took into account the number of times announcers mentioned John Hancock, and the amount of TV air-time during which the company name was on screen in pre-game promos and during the broadcast.

America West's sponsorship of the Phoenix Suns arena is worth $5 million to the company during the regular season – that is, America West's name is mentioned enough times during broadcasts to equal $5 million worth of commercial time each season. America West spent $26 million for the 30-year sponsorship. Over the 30-season agreement, America West might receive $150 million worth of exposure, not to mention the fact that the Phoenix Suns usually make the playoffs. Heaven forbid the Phoenix Suns should make it to the championship!

Local sports teams and events are great opportunities for a small business to accomplish several goals: motivating or rewarding employees, entertaining clients, or spreading the company's message to a targeted demographic group.

Local and community events that can be sponsored include: community and youth leagues, school programs, and road races. Little league baseball teams are almost always sponsored by local companies. These are financially undemanding ways of sponsoring within a community.

The following are some suggestions to owners and managers of teams to help promote their sport and teams for sponsors:

- Ensure high-quality competition and increased skills.
- Preserve traditions and image.
- Ensure spectator enjoyment and involvement.
- Encourage grassroots involvement.
- Increase your profile.
- Protect the welfare of athletes.
- Ensure exciting and safe environments for spectators.

- Protect intellectual property rights owned by the sport.
- Make sure sponsors' needs are being met.

It is very important for the sponsor and the sponsoree to work together throughout the term of a contract and beyond. Each sponsoring company has different requirements. Contracts are developed so that the requirements are met. Contract monitoring is necessary to make sure this happens. In the future, there will be an increasing number of joint ventures. Structuring a deal so that all parties are protected is also important.

Many companies pay large dollar amounts to sponsor an event. However, if they feel it is no longer beneficial, they will drop the contract at the end of its life. Currently there are companies that measure sponsorship effectiveness. Usually a contract will offer the sponsor a certain amount of signage, TV commercial time, and various promotions. If at the end of the contract a sponsor does not feel that it was beneficial, the event may have to find another sponsor, or it may no longer exist.

Regional Sports Report newsletter, based in Stamford, Conn., has some tips on this subject:

- To ask about how your business can get involved, call the marketing representatives of local sports teams, leagues, and events.

- Start small. An in-kind sponsorship, for instance, allows a business to donate T-shirts or other goods. You can always add to your promotion next year.

- Look for affordable visibility. Signage, program advertising, radio spots, and other advertising vehicles are often available at local sporting events.

- Create your own event. Many pro teams and some all-sports radio stations have alumni teams that tour for charity. Ask the team marketing representative if your customers can play against these local sports celebrities or arrange for a celebrity appearance at your business.

- Offer lessons with a professional as a contest prize.

So You Want To Be A Sponsor?

Here is an example of how the process works using a fictional food manufacturer that might want to market through mogul:

Your Product

Let's say the name of your product is Chilly Time Chili, a microwavable, single-serve "healthy" chili, priced a bit higher than its competition.

Your market

Research shows most sales come from health-conscious, affluent baby-boomers and college kids. Both groups think the product's convenience justifies its *premium* price, and most sales for a chili – a product that promises to "turn up your furnace" – are during the winter.

Your Problem

Your focus group shows that people love Chilly Time Chili once they taste it, but the brand has low consumer awareness. Worse, you can't reach your target consumers through supermarket sampling, because they don't shop there much. They opt instead to eat out, use convenience stores, or shop at supermarkets during odd hours. Finally, they don't bother with newspaper supermarket coupons.

Your Solution

You call a research firm that hooks up marketers and sports events. The research firm has a suggestion: skiing. It coincides with your selling season and attracts your target market: affluent baby-boomers and college kids who hit ski slopes for winter or spring break.

Your Commitment

Good news! Skiing and Chilly Time Chili are a winning team. You renew your sponsorship, add new events, and increase your sports marketing spending. But guess what? Event organizers know you're happy. A couple years later, they raise sponsorship fees (for an event you've helped make more successful) – or they bring in so many low-paying sponsors that you get lost in the clutter. That happens. Often, a sponsor gets involved three to five years, and that's it. The company comes and goes.

Your Sales

You've done skiing one season. Want to go again? Research firms will help you track results. For about $25,000, they'll interview fans at two events, a service that includes collecting fans' names at events and calling them weeks later for "a general marketing survey" – which, of course, includes questions about chili brands. Those findings are compared against a control group of consumers with similar demographic and "psychographic" profiles to see if skiing works for Chilly Time Chili.

Your Ante

The research firm suggests $75,000 would pay for product sampling at enough events to affect sales. Paying $100,000-$300,000 would pay for sampling, an official sponsorship, a little on-site entertainment, and support promotions, such as discounted event tickets with Chilly Time Chili boxtops. Start at $300,000, and support spending could extend to infinity.

Your Call

There are world-class men's or women's racing events, freestyle skiing, mogul skiing and grass-roots events for amateurs at venues ranging from obscure sites chosen for their terrain, to major resorts drawing big crowds. Researching an event is suggested to find the right consumer's "psychographics." Researchers will ask fans at events questions designed to find out whether they switch brands often, are "opinion shapers" who can influence other consumers, are loyal to certain brands, or if they acknowledge sports events and the sponsor's efforts.

By Stephen Conley, USA TODAY
Source: USA TODAY research; text by Michael Hiestand.

To promote events, obviously your options are either to hire an agency or to do it yourself. If you hire an agency, get a written estimate identifying all the services that will be provided. Make sure you are getting solid promotion. Also, keep all copies of correspondence and proposals.

For the promotion to pay off, it is best to have integrated elements, such as banners, radio, TV, and newspapers. Publicity will promote the sponsoring company and the event. Try to tie these elements into a neat package. For radio, you could run a contest directed at the consumer market, giving listeners an opportunity to win tickets to a sporting event. Each time the contest is announced, the company name would be announced as the sponsor. The tickets would be part of the overall package. This increases exposure in the local community. Integrating diverse media is a positive way to promote a sponsor benefit package.

When choosing an event to sponsor, one must integrate marketing, promotion, and advertising to achieve success. One of the most important marketing rules is to budget one marketing dollar for every sponsorship dollar. Long-range planning is essential and should not be overlooked. Failure to plan – or under-funding after the event has taken place – can severely limit return on the investment. Do not promote without commitment. Plan to promote before and after the event. Utilize the theme of the sponsored event, and as the event draws near, begin your own marketing plan and build on the event. Make sure you continue to market once the event is over. Utilize multi-market exposure to promote your company. Build long-term.

Companies choosing events need to understand their target markets. What often happens is that a sponsoring company has no strategy or objectives. Planning is essential for a sponsorship to be successful. If no objectives or strategies are developed, the sponsoring company gets lost in the event itself, and therefore does not benefit from the sponsorship. It is essential for companies to understand the nature of sponsorship and how it works. This begins with understanding the target market of the event, and the market the company is looking to capture. Companies need to devote time and energy toward strategic objectives before committing sponsorship money. Companies should not become involved for the love of sports, but for the benefits of sponsorship and visibility. The question to ask is: How can the company benefit and get the most out of this sponsorship?

Things to Consider Before Committing to Sponsoring Events.

- Will your company be visible in one form or another throughout the event?
- Does the event deliver a positive image for the company?
- Is the event local, national, global?
- Will the company gain high visibility to a target consumer group?
- How much traffic and visibility does the sponsored event offer the company?
- Does the event match your company's current prospective clients?

Profile the event and company and make sure it's a match. By match, I refer to demographics, values, and image. Once this is determined, look for events and sports that are compatible. This enables a company to analyze the potential return on its investment.

Contract monitoring is an innovation borrowed from the world of construction. If certain stages in the building process are not completed successfully, the whole process is suspect. The contract should identify pre- and post-event issues, thereby creating a solid foundation for the event.

Contracts are essential to bond the parties together. The contract should identify the returns required by each party, and the parties should monitor the contract from execution to finish until these goals are met.

Never sponsor an event blindly. Determine how you are measuring the results of your sponsorship dollar. Once the event is over and the fanfare has faded, analyze how your company, product, or service was affected. Did it increase retail traffic? Did it increase sales? Did it match your objectives? Always set your goals and expectations when going into sponsorship, because it is an investment. Figure out how you will determine your success. Sponsorship is a commitment that should not be taken lightly.

Is It Worth Being An Official Sponsor?

The appeal of an event determines the cost. For example, the NCAA Final Four, World Series, Super Bowl and Olympics are heavily sponsored. However, a sponsoring company can get lost in the event. The sponsors of the 1996 Olympiad did not fare poorly (see chart), although some were barely recognized. Second- and third-tier sponsorships are 50-75% less expensive than title sponsorships but can sometimes accomplish the same objectives.

Unaided Recall of Olympic Sponsors - March, 1996			
342 persons – Actual sponsors are underlined – Data supplied by Performance Research, Inc.			
Brand/Company	**Pct.**	**Brand/Company**	**Pct.**
Coca-Cola	36.0 %	Proctor & Gamble	2.6%
McDonald's	29.2	General Motors	2.6
Nike	13.7	Ford	2.3
Pepsi	13.5	IBM	2.3
Kodak	7.6	Hanes	2.3
Reebok	7.0	Chevrolet	2.0
AT&T	5.3	Gatorade	1.8
Budweiser	5.3	Snickers	1.8
Delta	3.9	UPS	1.8
Visa	3.8	Cannon	1.5
Adidas	3.5	Jeopardy	1.5
NationsBank	3.5	Wheaties	1.5

Companies, Brands the Public *Believes*
Are Olympic Sponsors - March, 1996

Percentages rounded off to nearest whole number. Actual sponsors
are <u>underlined</u>. Data supplied by Performance Research, Inc.

AIRLINES	
<u>Delta</u>	<u>61</u> %
United Airlines	55 %
American Airlines	47 %

COMPUTERS	
<u>IBM</u>	<u>67</u> %
Apple	37 %
Microsoft	37 %

QUICK DELIVERY	
Federal Express	59 %
<u>UPS</u>	<u>54 %</u>
USPS/Express Mail	31 %

RESTAURANTS	
<u>McDonald's</u>	<u>84</u> %
Burger King	54 %
Wendy's	32 %
Subway	16 %

RETAIL CHAINS	
Sears	47 %
JCPenney	46 %
Wal-Mart	45 %
<u>Home Depot</u>	<u>22 %</u>

BEER	
<u>Budweiser</u>	<u>66</u> %
Miller	38 %
Coors	31 %

CREDIT CARDS	
<u>Visa</u>	<u>71</u> %
American Express	53 %
MasterCard	47 %
Discover	35 %

PHOTO FILM	
<u>Kodak</u>	<u>84 %</u>
Fuji	39 %
Polaroid	39 %

Olympic sponsorship has become the main setting for stealth or ambush marketing. A company pays $40 million to become an Olympic sponsor, then its competitor utilizes individual athletes to promote and market other products, which confuses the public.

In 1994, Olympic sponsors randomly called 250 households and gauged their perceptions of which companies were official Olympic sponsors. Three out of the four companies that were mentioned were *not* official Olympic sponsors. Coca-Cola, a top sponsor, was mentioned frequently (43% of those polled). The following positions were held by Olympic broadcast advertisers that did not fork over the $40 million dollar price tag to gain the Olympic sponsorship status. When asked to identify the official fast food restaurant of the 1994 Olympics, 57% credited Wendy's, while only 37% chose McDonald's, (the official sponsor); 6% were undecided. Visa (IOC; top sponsor) received 63%; American Express received 32%. Visa fared well because it was, in fact, the official sponsor.

About one-fifth of those polled (19%) said that they select products from companies that are official sponsors. Twenty-eight percent of American viewers report that a company's Olympic involvement has either "somewhat" or an "extreme" impact upon their everyday purchase decisions. The purpose of these studies is to find out if the $40 million price tag is worth becoming an Official sponsor of the Olympics. If the Olympic committee does not figure out a way to monitor and fight against ambush marketing, companies will no longer pay $40 million for the "Official Olympic Sponsorship". This could pose a problem.

Coca-Cola spent $250 million on its sponsorship during the 1996 Olympic games in Atlanta. Corporations realize the commercial value of the Olympics. Companies capitalize on sporting events, teams, and individuals. Leagues have done an incredible marketing job and are strategically able to match businesses with sports. In 1996, approximately $13.5 billion were spent on sports sponsorship. (Performance Research)

Steps involved in planning a sponsored event:

The following is a sponsorship proposal for a golf tournament. This example illustrates some of the aspects involved when developing a tournament tied in with a sponsorship proposal. This breakdown is meant for a smaller, more local event. When setting up a tournament or event requiring sponsorship, the first step is figuring out a budget. Usually a budget involves many different facets. It is difficult to budget because so many things come up. That is one of the considerations one must realize when putting together a tournament or event. Here are the considerations involved when tailoring a budget for a sponsorship proposal.

BUDGET

1. Retainer fee, staff salaries, normal PR expenses
   - Event director
   - Event coordinator
   - Project director
   - Secretary
   - Tournament director
   - Normal PR expenses (writing press releases, telephone calls, messenger service, interviews, etc.)
   - Administrative cost
2. Production engineer
3. Lodging
4. Transportation
5. Advertisement
6. Security
7. Entertainment fees
8. Visual aid promotional materials

Design and structuring is designed to eliminate chaos, simply by assigning responsibilities. Always consider that a person's position may require more than that person is assigned, and sometimes less.

DESIGN AND STRUCTURING

All of the aforementioned ideas, programs and campaigns would be handled by associates with their appointed staff of professionals.

The association and their appointed staff of professionals will be secured by a letter of agreement. This spells out all the duties and details of services to be performed in staging and presenting the tournament or event.

A plan of action is part of the public relations process; one needs a way of getting the media involved and determining which media will be utilized to promote the event or tournament. Media outlets provide great opportunities to promote. Sometimes this requires a complete multimedia perspective, including radio, TV, newspapers, and billboards. A plan of action is useful in determining how the event will be promoted, what steps to be taken, and what contacts to make.

THE PLAN OF ACTION

A combination of national and local celebrities will participate in the first annual celebrity golf tournament. This tournament will draw amateur golfers from different cities across the country.

A gala hospitality party will be held during the weekend of the festival for the press, sponsors, and VIP guest. The event will be hosted with special entertainment and an elegantly catered buffet.

A statewide media blitz will be conducted, with a heavy emphasis upon AM and FM radio; public, commercial, and cable television; and various publications.

A souvenir book, free of charge, will be provided and distributed. The book will give community groups, private sponsors, and others an opportunity to advertise. It will also provide informative information about the celebrity participants, tournaments, and on- and off-stage activities.

GOVERNMENTAL SUPPORT

Several city and state agencies (e.g. the Office of Tourism Development, Department of Economic Development, Governor's Press Office, Mayor's Office, Bureau of Recreation and Parks, and Department of Highways and Traffic Control) have provided support in the past. In addition, the governor is expected to issue a proclamation declaring our event as the official salute to [unknown].

Now it's time to put everything to work and market the event. First, you need a budget for potential positions to be hired and an approximate amount of money you have to spend. Then you will need to figure out how to raise the funds for the event to be successful and profitable. This is where sponsorship packages need to be implemented. It is best to have several different sponsorship packages with varying dollar amounts. Make sure when putting proposals together that the potential sponsor knows exactly what is to be received. The reason you have a range of different sponsorships is to obtain larger sponsorship packages while not losing the smaller ones either. Often pending the event, sports terms are used to describe the sponsorship package. The following illustration uses a golf tournament as a sponsorship package.

Sponsorship Breakdown and Benefit Packages

GOLF TOURNAMENT HOLE OR TEE SPONSORSHIP $2,000

Any individual business or corporation wishing to assist the fundraising efforts of the program by sponsoring a hole or a tee in the golf tournament will receive the following for their sponsorship dollars:

> A. A business card-size ad in the souvenir program book.
>
> B. Company products in the "golfers' gift" bag.

GOLF TOURNAMENT SPONSOR $5,000

The sponsors of the golf tournament associated with this fundraising event will receive the following for their sponsorship dollars:

> A. Corporate mention on all promotional materials and press releases associated with the event. (This includes registration forms.)
>
> B. Corporate name or logo inscribed on all trophies awarded.

C. Special golf bags to be made up with sponsor's logo or name and given away as tournament gifts.

D. One full-page ad in the souvenir program book.

E. Five complimentary tickets to the hospitality party.

F. Corporate promotional items and products (if allowable) to be given to tournament players.

G. The right to post corporate banner plus product on golf course.

H. Community award recognizing your sponsorship.

SPONSORSHIP $50,000 (Partial) – $150,000 (Total)

A. Corporate mention with all promotional materials and press releases associated with the event and/or weekend

B. Corporate participation in the golf and tennis tournaments.

C. Corporate name or logo inscribed on all trophies awarded.

D. Corporate name or logo inscribed on all T-shirts, sun visors, and headbands.

E. Corporate name or logo inscribed on all tickets.

F. Corporate name or logo inscribed on all street banners,

G. Corporate name or logo inscribed on all posters and handbills.

H. One full-page ad in the souvenir program book.

I. Corporate banner on stages.

J. Sampling locations available for product distribution.

K. Corporate posters and logo hung in and around the field.

L. Community Award recognizing sponsorship.

A *sponsorship proposal* includes everything that will be done to promote the event or tournament. This is necessary so that a corporation or company will know the amount of effort being put forth on behalf of the event or tournament. Each time something is done to promote the event, this is recorded in the sponsorship proposal. The proposal states the importance and purpose for trying to raise money. It allows the potential sponsor to know why this event is happening. Usually to open the proposal, you will need to write a short introduction about the event or tournament. A purpose statement is a nice way to open.

SPONSORSHIP PROPOSAL

This golf tournament will feature athlete celebrities, as well as local artists joining together to raise money for a special purpose. It is aimed at members of the community for support and appreciation. The event is partially sponsored by one or more major corporations.

A multi-purpose marketing and promotional campaign is the best approach to enhance all interest in the staging and presenting of this event. Our suggested campaign would address itself to the following interest:

A. Give the sponsoring corporations a great direct consumer and minority community public relations vehicle.

B. Raise the visibility and awareness level of the sponsoring corporation's products.

C. Lend support toward increasing product sales and corporate images throughout the communities targeted for support of the special cause.

D. Create a goodwill corporate image expansion program throughout the area in a direct consumer visual aid form by identifying sponsors via banners, fliers, posters, stages, and tickets at major media events.

E. Provide advertising space in the official celebrity golf and tennis tournament publication.

F. Capture the attention of visitors to the state – as well as residents – for their support of the event.

G. Enhance the overall efforts of the entire program and the sponsoring corporations.

In the course of marketing and promoting this upcoming event, we would also address our efforts and attentions to the creative ends and aspects of the general advertising and promotional campaigns associated with such an event, including:

A. Radio station time buys and contests.

B. Writing and disbursement of press releases, stories, photos, etc. to the various media outlets to promote of the event.

C. Setting up interviews, press conferences, radio talk shows, TV appearances, etc. for participating artists and principals behind the creation of the event.

D. Creating the theme of the event, as well as the uniformity of all promotional pieces and visual aids associated with the planning and staging of the event. In the area of visual promotional aid, we think in terms of the following:

   1. T-shirts

   2. Posters and handbills

3. Street banners

4. Sun visors

5. Headbands

Finally, it is important to have rules. Rules allow the tournament to have a winner, and help to make the event move along at a smoother pace. Here are some rules you may want to incorporate for a golf tournament with guidelines for awards.

RULES

Maximum enjoyment of this golf tournament can be attained only if play moves at a reasonable pace. Golfers can play this tournament in less than four hours if they:

1. Are ready to hit the ball when it is their foursome's turn, and avoid unnecessary delays in playing their tournament round.

2. Try to help each member of their foursome spot where their ball landed during course of play.

3. Tee off as soon as the group in front of them is clear, and be sure their shot will not hit into the previous group's course.

4. Limit the search for each lost ball to five minutes. Anyone who spends more than five minutes searching for a lost ball will be disqualified from tournament trophy and prize competition.

5. Each tournament play must hole out, if their score is to be counted. No "gimmies" on any putts.

Electric carts are to be kept on asphalt or paved cart paths at tees and greens, and carts shall remain at least 30 feet from the greens.

AWARDS

- Tournament will be flighted and scored by the Calloway System in the following manner.

  A score of 72 and under   Championship Flight

  A score of 72 to 77   A Flight

  A score of 78 to 85   B Flight

  A score of 86 to 93   C Flight

A score of 94 and over   D Flight

- A blind hole scoring system will then determine the tournament score in the respective flight.

- First- and second-place winners in each flight will receive trophies.

- Trophies or a prize will be awarded to the following winners:

  * Overall low gross tournament player

  * _____ Drive

  * Closest to the pin (selected three-par hole)

  * Best dressed golfer

  * Worst tournament player

A limited field of 50 players are accepted for the celebrity/amateur golf tournament. Register early! Registrations are accepted only if player space is available an hour before tournament begins.

Finish Like a Pro

Finish like a pro as you tee off for (PURPOSE) at the Fifth annual celebrity golf tournament at the posh (LOCATION). Meet sports celebrities (FAMOUS ATHLETES), and media personalities Jaguar Myers, (FAMOUS NAMES), WWIN-TV 29 and

(NAMES), when you join a host of (PEOPLE) and corporate executives in an eventful day of enjoyment and relaxation.

The primary purpose of the tournament is to raise money for the (CHARITABLE FOUNDATION), which helps financially disadvantaged students receive an education. The challenge of this year's tournament is to exceed the (DOLLAR AMOUNT FROM LAST YEAR). When you play in the tournament, your financial donation directly helps (WHO IT HELPS) for the challenge of tomorrow.

As prime sponsor of the tournament, (SPONSOR) raised thousands of dollars to underwrite the expenses of the tournament. (ORGANIZATION)'s unrivaled excellence is why (SPONSOR) has sponsored the tournament since its inception in 1984. (SPONSOR)'s colossal support of the tournament is only a small part of its ongoing commitment to (PURPOSE) and to serving the community.

As host of the tournament since 1984, the (HOST) seeks other prominent corporations to participate as associate sponsors.

The challenge of this year's tournament is to exceed the (DOLLAR AMOUNT) raised in (YEAR). Contribute to that challenge by joining the increasing number of (ORGANIZATIONS) that participate in the tournament each year.

Par For The Course

Experience the sheer enjoyment of golfing with (HOSTING ORGANIZATION) and sports and media celebrities. Indulge yourself in these on-the-course amenities:

- Opportunity to meet sports and media celebrities.
- Golf package includes:
  Green fees, cart, favors, clubhouse, locker facilities, and valet parking.
- 1st, 2nd, 3rd, and 4th place prizes will be awarded.
- Door Prizes
- Closest-to-the-pin prizes
- Continental breakfast
  Chilled juices, assorted fresh Danish, freshly brewed coffee, and hot tea.
- Mini press conference
  Meet tournament officials and celebrities.
- Tee-off – shotgun start, scramble format
- Refreshments served on the golf course
- Electrifying entertainment
- Relax at a gala outdoor cocktail-buffet reception upon completion of your winning game.

- Program will be held and prizes awarded at the reception.

NASCAR Racing Sponsorship

One of the benefits of sponsoring auto racing is consumer loyalty (see chart). The advantage of signage and sponsorship is both TV time and spectatorship of the racing event. NASCAR Winston Cup has the highest television exposure, which includes 44 telecasts, 529 NASCAR Winston Cup sponsors, and $419 million worth of exposure. (NASCAR fans across the country by Performance Research)

Except a Politician!

Race fans were asked to identify from a list of hypothetical sponsors, which sponsors were, in their opinion, completely inappropriate as a sponsor of the Winston Cup car.

Ranking dead last – below the sins of "condoms," "*Penthouse Magazine*," "Absolut Vodka," and "Mitsubishi televisions" – were "politicians." As much as 83% of fans ranked them as completely inappropriate NASCAR sponsors.

This is not to say that NASCAR fans are not supportive to their sponsors. On the contrary, according to Jed Pearsall, president of Performance Research, "NASCAR fans provide one of the highest levels of brand loyalty and sponsorship support of any one of the hundred or so sports and special events we've tested."

In this study – which involved interviews with over 1,000 random nationwide NASCAR fans – over one-half (57%) indicated that they had a "higher" trust in products offered by NASCAR sponsors. In comparison, only 16% of the general public holds a "higher" trust in Olympic sponsors, and only 5% have a "higher" trust in sponsors of World Cup soccer.

In addition, nearly three-fourths of the NASCAR audience (71%) reported that they "almost always" or "frequently" choose a product involved in NASCAR over another product, simply because of the sponsorship. In comparison, only 52% of professional tennis enthusiasts, and 47% of PGA golf enthusiasts, "almost always" or "frequently" chose products based on sponsorships.

RaceStat, the syndicated NASCAR research project generating these results, was funded by corporate sponsors seeking an unbiased look at the NASCAR audience, and RaceStat is not affiliated with NASCAR. In this over 100-page report, marketers can access information including demographics, product usage and ownership data, lifestyle interests, and numerous sponsorship measures, such as unaided sponsor awareness, coupon interests,

94

coupon redemption frequencies, and other data critical to NASCAR marketing. Will the real NASCAR fan please stand up?

According to the study, nationwide NASCAR fans can be described predominantly as male (78%), married (73%), with an average age of 42 years. They own homes (81%), with 3.4 cars per household. The median household income range is between $35,000 and $50,000, and almost all are employed full time (87%).

Some of this may contradict NASCAR's internal data, which indicates there is a higher ratio of females in its audience. But according to Bill Doyle, RaceStat's project coordinator, 'NASCAR's figures are typically collected on-site (at the races) and show a higher percentage of females. Although this information is correct for those attending races, it does not accurately describe the comprehensive audience nationwide, which provides a greater number of "occasional or moderate" male NASCAR fans. Marketers must decide which of the several different NASCAR segments to target – on-site, nationwide, or regional, and with a "low," "medium," or "high" interest level – and then identify the appropriate research.'

What does this mean to NASCAR marketers? Corporations no longer have to sponsor Dale, Rusty, Darrell, or Kyle just on instinct. Now there is proof!

The following proposal is broken down into the following components:

- Naming rights
- Hospitality
- Season-long signage
- Media promotion
- Consumer promotion

Here are the benefits and sponsor breakdown for NASCAR Winston Cup Series. The pricing for the three-year entitlement:

Year	$ Pricing
1997	$650,000
1998	$700,000
1999	$750,000

Naming Rights

- Sponsors and events' names and logos will be combined and can be used in promotions.

Hospitality

- 300 tickets located in a prime grandstand area

- 100 grandstand tickets to the NAPA 500 (NASCAR Winston Cup, Nov. 1997)

- 300 grandstand tickets to the Busch Light 300 (Busch Grand National, March 1997)

- 300 general admission tickets to the General Tire/Hoosier 500 (Automobile Racing Club of America, Nov. 1997)

- Use of 55-person luxury suite (located in the east turn grandstand), for each of six yearly Speedway events (food and beverage are extra)

- Use of furnished hospitality area for 300 guests (food and beverage are extra) for the sponsored Winston Cup Event

Season-long signage

- One 10' x 30' track-side billboard

- Prominent exposure on the state-of-the-art, front-entrance, four-colored Matrix Message Center

- Sponsor logo on flags at Speedway front entrance

- Victory Lane signage on the backdrop

- Signage at other negotiable locations (e.g. logo on grass in turn one, tunnel, signage, outside billboards, etc.)

Media Promotion

- Full-page, four-colored program ad and a one-page editorial

- Option to enter sponsor logo vehicles in the parade laps for the March and November events

- Display booth in high-traffic area

- Logo on official apparel (T-shirts, sweatshirts, hats, etc.)

Consumer Promotion

- Creation of store-level ticket giveaways, contests, and apparel programs

Joyce Julius & Assoc., a research firm, conducted a study to analyze the national television exposure sponsors receive. The study included "mentions", in-focus camera exposure of logos, and company names on cars. The monetary values are calculated based on the cost of commercial advertising during the broadcast. This study encompasses the first half of the 1996 racing season. Take into consideration that a winning team or driver will get more exposure. The DuPont Co. received great air time. Their driver is Jeff Gordon, who at the time of the study was the point leader. DuPont received five hours, 38 minutes and 26 seconds of screen time, and was also mentioned 87 times.

Racing League	Telecasts	Sponsors	Total Exposure Value
NASCAR Winston Cup	44	29	$418,882,045
PPG Indy Car World Series	25	358	$100,785,920
NASCAR Busch Series	21	643	$83,152,010
NASCAR Craftsman Truck	15	542	$64,557,125
NHRA	23	464	$25,925,615

The following charts illustrate the average fan who is active in NASCAR racing. Demographics include gender, household income, age, and education. Demographic research is used by sponsors and advertisers as a focus for a product or service. The charts are used to help evaluate the average fan. This can also be a measure for buying power, within a consumer market.

Simmons Market Research Bureau and Performance Research.

Auto racing has the largest following, and its fans are notorious for loyalty to sponsored brands. (see chart)

COMPARATIVE SPONSOR LOYALTY

Based on independent 1992-1996 research reports of over 200 self-proclaimed fans of each sport. Percentage of fans within each sport who claim to purchase a sponsor's product over a non-sponsor's product "almost always" or "frequently."

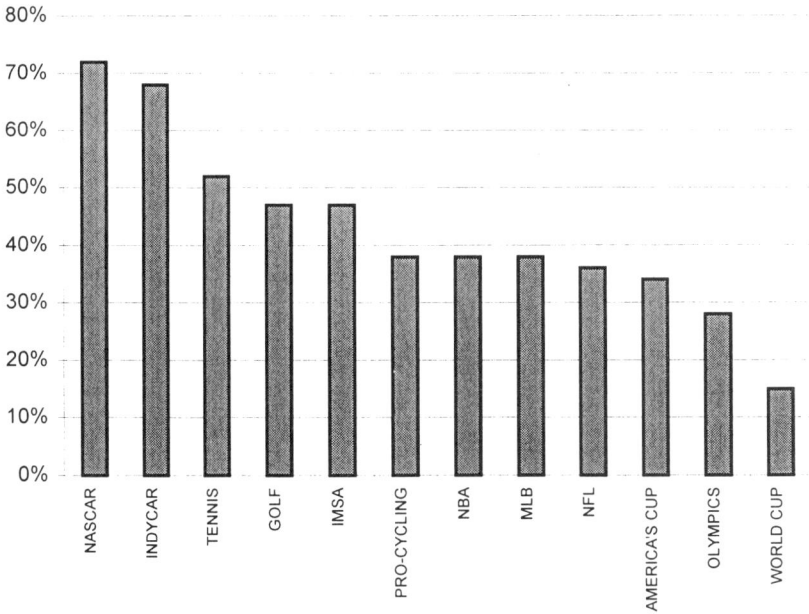

The following bar graph illustrates the age demographic of a NASCAR fan:

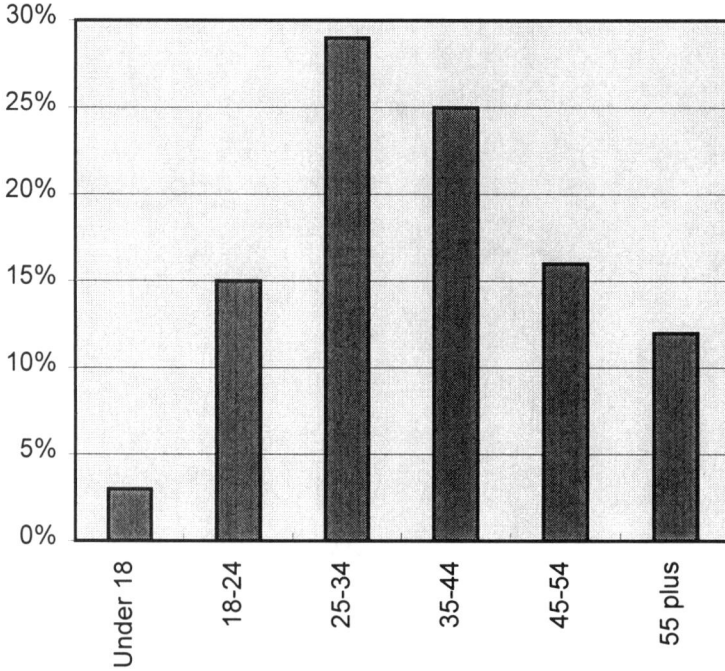

These graphs are demographic breakdowns for NASCAR auto racing. An advertiser would use these graphs to make sure the demographics hit the company's target market. Sponsors would also use this information for the same purpose.

GENDER

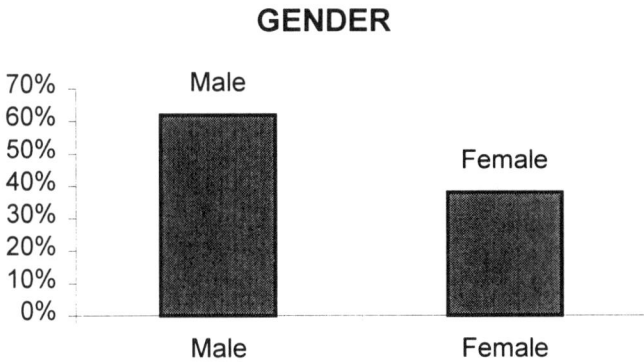

HOUSEHOLD INCOME

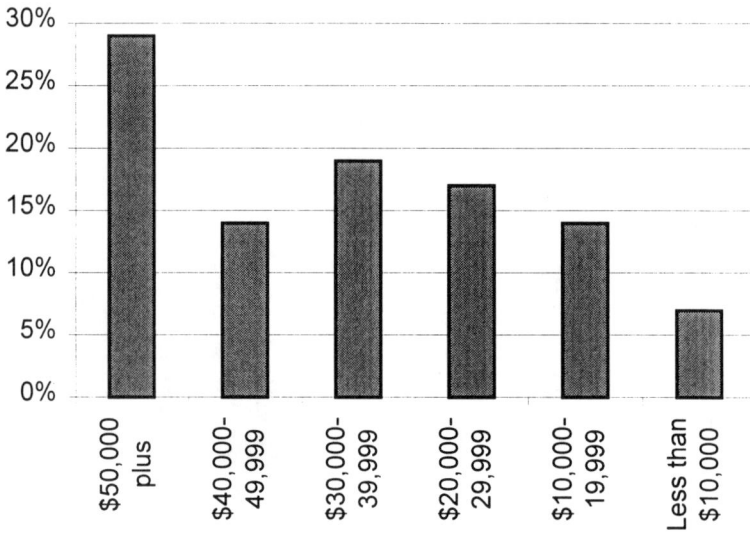

Source: Simmons Market Research Bureau and Performance

The impressive number here is that nearly a third of NASCAR fans make over $50,000, while 60% earn over $30,000. The significance is the buying power of NASCAR fans.

For educational demographics, 88% of NASCAR fans have a high school diploma or better.

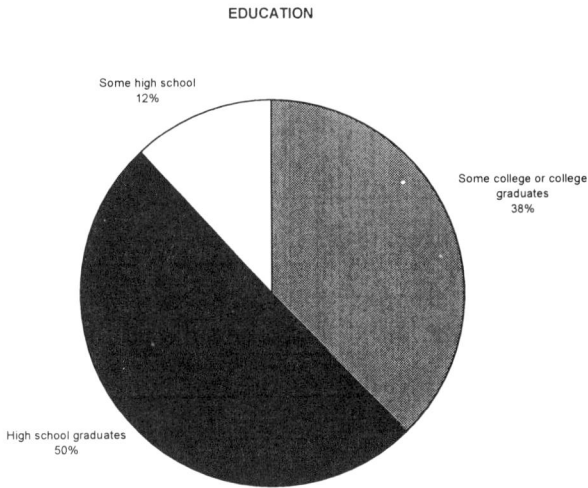

EDUCATION

Some high school
12%

Some college or college
graduates
38%

High school graduates
50%

(Reprinted with permission. Ernie Saxton's Motorsports Sponsorship Marketing News: Ernie Saxton Communications, !448 Hollywood Ave., Langhorne, PA 19047 (215) 752-7797. ($69.95/year for subscription.)

Americans Believe...

Americans overwhelmingly believe corporate sponsorships are beneficial for events and host communities, and they say government should stay out of regulating corporate support of sports and entertainment events.

Those were findings of the public's attitudes survey released by the American Coalition for Entertainment and Sports Sponsorship (ACESS). The nationwide poll, conducted March 14-17 by Roper Starch Worldwide, surveyed 1,010 adults over the age of 18.

The survey concludes that 80% of Americans believe that corporate sponsorship is significantly important as a source of money for professional sports. Seventy-four percent agreed that corporate sponsorship provides benefits to the communities in which the events occur.

"Americans see corporate sponsorship as a very important way to promote events," said Humpy Wheeler, president and general manager of Charlotte Motor Speedway and an advisory board member of ACESS. "They know that sponsorship helps promoters keep events affordable, attract spectators, and put on a high-quality show."

"Successful local events, in turn, help the economies of host communities and give out-of-town spectators a positive, lasting impression of an area. Obviously, Americans see the important link between sponsorship and event success."

Considering the public's supportive views of sponsorship, Wheeler said it is not surprising that Americans are skeptical of governmental regulation of such events.

In the poll, 74% of Americans questioned said government should have little or no influence on the types of companies that sponsor professional events. A clear majority – nearly four out of five – felt that the businesses involved with putting on professional sports events should have the most influence on the types of companies that sponsor them.

In addition, 69% of those surveyed said they oppose governmental efforts to prevent certain companies from sponsoring sports events.

"Americans feel that the current system provides the best mechanism to make decisions about event sponsorship," Wheeler said. "After all, facility owners and managers are in the best position to understand all of the elements that go into a successful event. They also understand what's at stake in the local community.

"Americans agree, government should have no role in these decisions."

ACESS is a national non-profit organization dedicated to promoting and protecting the benefits of corporate sponsorship of sports and entertainment events. Members include sanctioning bodies, event promoters, sponsor companies, sports figures, and fans.

Stadium Sponsorship

In the '90s, sponsorship has become a hot topic. Each year, billions of dollars are spent on sponsorship. Stadiums are now being sponsored: The United Center in Chicago and the Fleet Center are two examples. LM Ericsson, Inc., spent $20 million over 10 years in order to become the stadium sponsor for the Carolina Panthers. The Brendan Byrne arena has become the Continental Airlines Arena at the New Jersey Meadowlands. Continental Airlines spent millions of dollars to replace the name of the facility.

Pro Player, a division of Fruit-of-the-Loom, paid $20 million over 10 years to replace the name Joe Robbie in the title of the stadium that is home to the Miami Dolphins and Florida Marlins.

Costly Building Boom

More than $4 billion has been spent on sports arenas, with $7 billion more expected to be spent in the near future.

Facility/team

Stadium	$Cost	Year Built	Public/Private
Skydome Toronto Blue Jays	**$600**	1989	P/P
TWA Dome **at America's Center** St. Louis Rams	290	1995	Public
Molson Centre**** Montreal Canadians	230	1996	Private
Coors Field Colorado Rockies	215	1995	Public
Georgia Dome Atlanta Falcons	214	1992	Public
CoreStates Center Philadelphia Flyers/76ers	210	1996	Private
Orioles Park **at Camden Yards** Baltimore Orioles	210	1992	Public
Corel Center **(Palladium)** Ottawa Senators	200	1996	P/P
The Ballpark **in Arlington** Texas Rangers	191	1994	P/P
Alamodome San Antonio Spurs	186	1993	Public
GM Place Vancouver Canucks/Grizzlies	180	1995	Private

United Center*** Chicago Blackhawks/Bulls	**180**	1994	Private
Jacobs Field Cleveland Indians	**168**	1994	P/P
San Jose Arena San Jose Sharks	**163**	1993	P/P
Fleet Center **160** Boston Celtics/Bruins		1995	Private
Gund Arena **155** Cleveland Cavaliers		1994	P/P
Comiskey Park Chicago White Sox	**150**	1991	Public
Rose Garden Portland Trail Blazers	**145**	1995	P/P
Gator Bowl* Jacksonville Jaguars	**136**	1995	Public
Marine Midland Arena Buffalo Sabres	**128**	1996	P/P
Arrowhead Pond **of Anaheim** Anaheim Mighty Ducks	**120**	1993	P/P
Ice Palace Tampa Bay Lightning	**120**	1996	P/P
Target Center Minnesota Timberwolves	**104**	1990	P/P
America West Arena Phoenix Suns	**101**	1992	P/P

Orlando Arena Orlando Magic/Solar Bears	100	1989	P/P
Kiel Center St. Louis Blues	99 +	1994	Private
Bradley Center Milwaukee Bucks	80	1988	Private
Ericsson Stadium Carolina Panthers	70	1996	Private
Palace of Auburn Hills Detroit Pistons	70	1988	Private
Charlotte Coliseum Charlotte Hornets	58	1988	Public
Delta Center Utah Jazz	55 +	1991	Private
Miami Arena Miami Heat/Florida Panthers	52	1988	P/P
Arco Arena Sacramento Kings	40	1988	Private

P/P=Public/Private Partnership. * Includes, among other items, land, site preparation, construction, and administration costs. ** Canadian dollars. *** Renovations to existing facility. **** Canadian dollars, excluding land costs. ***** $180 million is the approximate construction cost (excluding other expenses) + Debt outstanding.
SOURCE: Fitch Investors Service.

The Ford Motor Company spent $40 million to be the naming sponsor for the new dome being built to house the Detroit Lions. The Lions are currently partially owned by the Ford family. William Clay Ford, who is part owner of the team, proposed a

multiple sponsorship deal with the Big Three auto makers –
Chrysler and General Motors teaming up with the Ford Motor
Company. This was an effort to raise $50 million in private funds
to build a new dome.

During the 1996 Final Four, the name change at the Meadowlands
was a cause of great controversy. The TV station that was licensed
to broadcast the event decided not to call the arena by its proper
name, Continental Airlines Arena. Continental was upset over the
loss of publicity. Obviously, it was upsetting to Continental
because the company had paid millions of dollars to have the arena
renamed, and each time the TV station used the "Meadowlands
Arena," it was one less mention of Continental's company name.
Continental lost out.

Another source of controversy regarding sponsorship comes out of
Dallas. Dallas Cowboys maverick owner Jerry Jones signed AT&T
as the official telecommunications sponsor of Texas Stadium. The
official telecommunications company of the NFL is Sprint. Sprint
inked a three-year deal for $100 million with the league. Jones's
deal with AT&T is for three years and a reported $6 million. Jerry
Jones has not been pleased with the NFL properties revenue-
sharing agreement. Jones feels his team should receive a larger
portion of the revenue, because Dallas Cowboys-related
merchandise accounted for nearly 25% of all NFL merchandise

sold over the past two seasons. The revenue of the Sprint deal gives each team $800,000. Jones's agreement with AT&T would have brought in an extra $1.2 million per season. Another move Jones made to upset the NFL was his signing with other non-official NFL sponsors, such as Pepsi, Nike, American Express, and Dr. Pepper.

In September of 1995, the NFL tried to sue Jones for $300 million, claiming his sponsorships violated the revenue-sharing policy. Jones in turn sued the NFL for $750 million. The revenue-sharing policy allows that the money being made by NFL licensees is split evenly among the 30 teams. In 1995, the revenue brought in $3.15 billion.

JC Penney is a sponsor of the NHL. However, the department store has not been as visible as other NHL sponsors. JC Penney raffled off the honor of taking home the Stanley Cup. The contest was the first of its kind. This is an example of how to maintain a positive relationship when two sides work together. It was the first time JC Penney ran a promotion with the NHL on a national level.

A Bold Prediction For the Future

The future of sports may be affected by individual and team sponsors. Think about this: Soccer is really the first team sport where players can wear sponsor patches on their uniforms. The future could bring similar liberalized policies in other sports, as sponsorship demands increase for basketball, football, and baseball. Picture this: Michael Jordan dribbling up the court in his Chicago Bulls uniform with Gatorade, LDDS Long Distance, and Nike patches. Barry Sanders could be wearing a McDonald's patch, Ken Griffey Jr. an Upper Deck and a Pizza Hut patch. Players may become sponsor billboards in the future. With salaries escalating into the $100-million range, the money has to come from somewhere. So why not the sponsors? The teams don't know when to say "no" which may result in over-saturation of the market. Owners and players are pushing the limits. How else will these outrageous salaries be paid? Higher ticket prices will drive fans away. Sponsors have access to millions, which could assist in paying these salaries. Think about it.

Sports Services of America™ surveyed fans regarding their feelings about individuals wearing sponsorship patches to promote sponsoring companies or for athlete endorsements. Seventy-eight

percent saw nothing wrong with it. <u>Will athletes become walking
billboards?</u>

Chapter 4

Promotion

Bill Veeck revolutionized promotion with mixed success. Veeck was a promotion visionary, but not all of his promotions were successful. In fact, two of them resulted in game forfeits.

In 1974 at Cleveland's Municipal Stadium, a promotion called "10-cent Beer Night" brought in a lot of fans, but resulted in fan rioting. The Indians had to forfeit the game. In 1979 at Chicago's Comiskey Park, the "Disco Demolition" night, which took place on the field between a double-header with the Detroit Tigers, resulted in fans bringing in disco albums to be burned and blown up. What began as an innocent promotion turned into a nightmare. The Chicago White Sox were forced to forfeit the second game of the doubleheader due to fan rioting.

Veeck was an innovator, and he is responsible for the exploding scoreboards to celebrate home runs. He is also responsible for athletes' names being put on the backs of jerseys, and the ivy at Chicago's Wrigley Field. Veeck once allowed fans to manage a game by holding up decision cards.

On Sept. 25, 1946, Veeck then the owner of the Cleveland Indians, offered free admission to a game against the Chicago White Sox with only 12,800 in attendance. In 1951, he purchased the St. Louis Browns. A week later, Eddie Gaedel – "The Midget from St. Louis" – stepped up to the plate. Gaedel walked. American League president Will Harridge was not amused. Veeck had an imaginative mind, constantly trying to come up with new ideas to increase fan interest. He paved the way for modern-day promotions.

Generally, there are two types of stadium event promotions: in-stadium and walk-in.

In-stadium promotions occur inside the stadium, and could involve something as random as a lucky seat giveaway. If a person has the ticket for a randomly drawn seat, the person wins a pizza or a trip to spring training. The promotion adds enjoyment to the game and gives the fans something to cheer about. Other in-stadium promotions include children racing against a mascot, an event the child usually wins. Events can create a more cheerful atmosphere for the fans.

As for walk-in promotions, "Bat Day" is usually a winner. The first 10,000 people to attend will receive a bat, compliments of the sponsor, Louisville Slugger. There is a "Hat Day" as well, which is sponsored by a local sponsor, Jim's Auto Body. Promotions and minor league baseball have often been synonymous. Some teams have up to 50 promotional giveaways in a season. Sponsors can range from U.S. Air to Pepsi-Cola, and items can range from vacation giveaways to beach towels.

Promotions make the atmosphere more enjoyable and also give fans a chance to walk away with souvenirs. Minor league baseball has taken promotions to another level. In Trenton, N.J., the Trenton Thunder of the AA Eastern League hold a Fan Appreciation Night/ Car Giveaway during their final home game. One lucky fan actually drives away with a car. This elaborate giveaway is sponsored by a local car dealer.

Awareness of the Negro leagues has been heightened in recent years. Several minor-league teams have held a Negro League night promotion. On one particular night, former Negro League players gathered and signed autographs. The fans got the opportunity to salute the men who paved the way for integration but in the past never received recognition for their efforts.

The AAA Colorado SkySox run a promotion in which judges choose the messiest interior of a car in the parking lot, and the winner receives a baseball hat and some Armor All Spot and Wash. The South Bend Silver Hawks of the single-A Midwest League held a "Pamper Yourself Night." The team brought in hair-stylists and masseuses to work on the fans. The Memphis Chicks of the AA Southern League teamed up with Cecil's Supermarket to create Cecil's Supermarket Lobster Night. The first 1,000 fans at the game were given live lobsters. They could either take them home or have them cooked at the game. Possibly the most unusual promotion ever planned was the independent Western League's Palm Spring Suns' "Clothing Optional Night," in which their fans would have gotten the opportunity to watch a game in the nude. Unfortunately, due to a conflict this event never happened.

Minor league teams realize that promotions make the game fun and bring in spectators. Minor League Baseball and other sports are usually less inventive, and sometimes gear their promotions more toward families. Ticket prices for major league games in all sports are continually being raised. A minor league game offers the same excitement at a more affordable price. Such promotions have not gone unnoticed by the major leagues.

The Los Angeles Kings once made a guarantee to their season ticket holders. Customers who were not satisfied with the team's performance would be a refund of the season ticket price. The catch: This offer was only good the first week of the season. The Chicago Cubs came up with "Seventies Night," which brought 36,766 fans wearing bell-bottoms, hip-huggers, and platform shoes.

The atmosphere of sports has changed dramatically over time, with the entrance into stadiums of such innovations as "Stadium Click Effects" by Sound Creations – a product that highlights game action with sound effects and animation. An example would be the sound of a shattering window when a foul ball is hit. The Famous Chicken integrates this type of system into his routines. The purpose of the "Stadium Click Effects" computer system is to utilize sound effects and accentuate the action simply by clicking a button. The system holds music, sound effects, and video, so an image can be seen over the video screen while sound effects play. Minor league teams, as well as major league teams in all sports, utilize this system to create a more fan-friendly atmosphere.

Finding the Right Sport with which to Promote Your Product

Businesses research a sport to narrow down the demographics of its fans. They want to reach the right consumers to target their products or services toward.

The importance of finding the right sport to promote your product is imperative. There are many factors to consider. The most important concept: <u>know your customers</u>. Get to know who your market is. This can be done through surveys. Understand their likes and dislikes by having an idea about your average customer. Determine the following facts: their household income, age, hobbies, and anything that helps you key in. First you may survey your customers to focus in on demographics. A survey can be done over the phone, by mail, or by fax. Remember, if you are advertising nationally, the sports your customers choose to associate with may differ from state to state, or between climate settings. When choosing a sport to associate with, you need to look at the exposure of the sport or event; this can be a key factor in your choice.

You may need to break your survey up in regions based on climate, state, etc., depending on the promotional budget and location. The amount of money you are spending on your promotion will determine how specific you will be in your survey.

In many cases, sports marketing firms such as Sports Services of America™ will already have information similar to what you are looking for on file, having gathered information from previous surveys and reports.

Sample Questions

1. Which sport do you watch most?

2. How long have you been watching this sport?

3. What is your second-most-watched sport?

4. How long have you been watching that sport?

5. How often do you attend live sporting events?

6. What are some of the reasons you don't attend?

7. How often do you watch sporting events on television?

8. What type of promotion, if any, would entice you to go to a live event?

An example of a product matching up with a team is Samsonite and the Pittsburgh Steelers. In the late 1970s – the glory years for the Steeler championships – the team matched up with Samsonite luggage. Commercials showed Steeler players trying to beat up the luggage. They ran on the luggage, threw it, and basically pounced on it. The purpose of the ad was to illustrate how tough Samsonite luggage is. This was a good approach by Samsonite. At the end of the commercial, it showed the Steelers worn out and the luggage still looking great. A promotion accompanying this commercial could have utilized autographed memorabilia, such as a team-autographed Samsonite suitcase. An example of a connected promotion would be a drawing in which fans won tickets to an away game and received free luggage, all expenses paid, or won a suitcase with the Steeler logo.

The following are some statistics on the sports, athletes, and teams considered favorites by the fans. (Sports Services of America):

- Favorite professional team sport
     NFL football
- Favorite professional teams (any major league)
     1) Dallas Cowboys
     2) Chicago Bulls

- Favorite professional athletes

     1) Michael Jordan
     2) Joe Montana
     3) Emmitt Smith
     4) Troy Aikman
     5) Shaquille O'Neal.
- Favorite NFL team
     1) Dallas Cowboys
     2) San Francisco 49ers
- Favorite NBA team
     1) Chicago Bulls
     2) Boston Celtics
- Favorite MLB team
     1) Atlanta Braves

2) New York Yankees
- Favorite NHL team
    1) Los Angles Kings
    2) New York Rangers
- Favorite professional team (any major league)
    1) Dallas Cowboys
    2) Chicago Bulls
- Favorite college sports program
    1) Notre Dame University
    2) University of Michigan
- Top college logo on clothing
    1) Notre Dame University
    2) University of Michigan

Favorite Professional Teams:

Dallas Cowboys	28%
Chicago Bulls	14%
San Francisco 49ers	12%
Atlanta Braves	10%
New York Giants	6%
Washington Redskins	6%
Miami Dolphins	6%
Kansas City Chiefs	6%
Buffalo Bills	6%
Oakland Raiders	6%
	100%

Favorite Professional Team Sport

NFL Football	51%
MLB Baseball	21%
NBA Basketball	18%

NHL Hockey	7%
no preference	3%
	100%

Most Hated Professional Teams

Dallas Cowboys	17%
L.A. Raiders	5%
Washington Redskins	3%
Buffalo Bills	2%
San Francisco 49ers	2%
Chicago Bulls	2%
Denver Broncos	2%
New York Yankees	2%
Detroit Pistons	2%
Philadelphia Eagles	1%
	100%

Product Promotion Using an Athlete

One example of the many sports promotions Sports Services of America has provided customers was an appearance by Joe Morris, New York Giant running back, for 1-800-COLLECT. The appearance was designed to increase visibility, tie in to a certain lifestyle, and build community support. There wasn't enough security to hold the crazed fans back. Joe described the experience as being an apple tree and having 200 people plucking at you all at once. Sports Services of America sent a press clipping to 200 media outlets in the local area, contacted the trade show organizers, and hung huge posters advertising that Joe Morris would appear at booth #336 from 3-5 p.m.

In this case, the customer was a long-distance telephone company looking to increase its visibility by a factor of 10 in two hours. We provided an athlete for 1-800-COLLECT's booth at a local New York exhibit and increased the company's visibility by 100 times. Normally they were getting 20 people per hour to stop at their booth. They had 400 people stop by their booth in the two hours Joe Morris was present, not to mention the intangibles of having a winning sports celebrity associated with their product. Some people in the local area were not at first familiar with the national long-distance telephone company. However, they were familiar with Joe Morris.

1-800-COLLECT - It's Fast. It's Easy. It Saves. Joe Morris of the New York Giants.

Joe Morris is a great person – the perfect person to host a sports promotion. I highly recommend him to all of my clients, especially in the New York area. Joe's business experience was made apparent by the way he handled the situation. He was calm, assuring the crowd that every person would get to meet him even if it meant he had to stay until closing. He enjoys working with the public, and it became obvious that not only is Mr. Morris an outstanding athlete, but he is a very pleasant person to be around. Morris even brought extra photos to sign.

In 1982, Joe Morris was drafted by the New York Giants in the second round. He was used sparingly in his first two NFL seasons, and no one was certain if Joe Morris would live up to his potential. But after he secured the starting running back job halfway through the '84 season, Joe would only see success in front of him. In his first starting assignment, Joe equaled a Giants' club record with three touchdowns against the Redskins, then reached his first 100-yard game (he ran for 107) versus the Cardinals. Joe went on a one-man rampage in 1985 and 1986, totaling 2,852 yards and 35 touchdowns. In the Giants' Super Bowl season of 1986, Joe played back-to-back 181-yard games in crucial wins over the Cowboys and Redskins. All told, seven of Joe's eight 100+ games took place in the last 10 games of the season. He continued to dominate games throughout the playoffs and Super Bowl, rushing for 313 yards in three games, including a 159-yard, two-touchdown effort in the opening playoff romp over the 49ers. In 1988, Joe rushed for a club record third 1,000-yard season, running for 1,083 yards.

Joe's career total of 5,296 yards moved him past Alex Webster and made him the Giants all-time leader in rushing. In all, Joe holds nine Giants career rushing records, along with two Pro Bowl and All-NFL honors from '85 and '86. Originally from North Carolina, Joe played college football at Syracuse, where he broke all the school's rushing records. He erased the records of former greats like Jim Brown, Larry Csonka, and Floyd Little, and he was an All-American in his senior year. Joe is active in the New York tri-state business community and is a highly visible public figure. He resides in New Jersey and has two daughters, Samantha and Blake.

Wednesday's Woman *Inside*

The New York Beacon

Showing the Way to Truth and Justice

Vol.3 No.22   June 6 — June 12, 1996   60 Cents

6 Banking   June 6 - June 12, 1996   *The New York Beacon*

Thousands At Black Expo Made Free 1-800 Collect Calls

1-800-Collect continued its support of the African-American community, as a national sponsor of Black Expo USA '96 at the Coliseum. Free 1-800 Collect long distance calls were offered to anywhere in the U.S., Puerto Rico and the Virgin Islands.

All-time New York Giant's leading rusher Joe Morris was at the booth taking photos and signing autographs for his fans.

"We are thrilled to be a part of Black Expo USA and wish to thank the African-American community for their support of 1-800-Collect," said Patty Proferes of 1-800 Collect. Black Expo USA provides a tremendous opportunity to make a close connection with this important consumer group. Also, we are pleased that through the donation of Black Expo USA tickets and 1-800-Collect t-shirts, dozens of people from Medgar Evers College were able to attend the event.

New York Giant leading rusher Joe Morris makes a call at the Black Expo USA

The copy of the newspaper article above is an example of the bottom line in using a sports celebrity for a promotion or grand opening. The visibility, goodwill, and credibility of athletes like Joe Morris create positive images in the public's eye about products or services with which these athletes are associated. People are more likely to believe in something that is printed in a newspaper, in a form, or in a non-paid advertisement rather than in a paid advertisement.

Nike's P.L.A.Y - Participate in the Lives of America's Youth.
John McEnroe, tennis player.

Nike's P.L.A.Y. - Participate in the Lives of America's Youth. Jimmy
Conners, tennis player.

1-800-COLLECT - It's Fast. It's Easy. It Saves. Dwayne Joseph of the Chicago Bears.

Chapter 5

Endorsements

Athletes can be used to market a wide range of products and services, such as leagues, card companies, and shoe manufacturers. Shoe companies are notorious for marketing and endorsing athletes. Sports Services of America™ marketing surveys have shown that product endorsements by sports celebrities have increased the value of products by more than 25% over the products of non-endorsed competitors.

Endorsement essentially is approval of a product or service – an agreement or partnership between the athlete and the manufacturer or company.

Endorse: To express approval or support publicly. To designate oneself as payee of a check by signing. To make good on an item.

When an athlete signs an endorsement contract, he becomes a business partner of the endorsee.

Endorsee: The company that represents and produces the products or services that are being endorsed.

Endorsement agreements are not license agreements. Endorsement means someone is giving his or her "stamp of approval" to a particular product, service, or company. A license agreement grants a manufacturer the right to make something using a registered trademark, a logo, a symbol, or an individual image and name.

What do marketers look for in an athlete?

1. Winning/success
2. Major media attraction (visibility)
3. Work ethic

The most important characteristic is an athlete's performance on the court or field. What an athlete does during competition is essential to his or her endorsement possibilities. Success is the #1 reason people associate with an athlete; therefore, marketers must capitalize on the athlete's popularity and championship image to capture the hearts of consumers.

There are companies that assist athletes with their image and then try to market the athletes to big companies. The aim of this approach is to get athlete endorsement deals by approaching a company rather that waiting for the company to approach the athlete. The athlete's image should not be underestimated. Dennis Rodman has created a niche for himself based on his image. As Rodman has dramatically demonstrated, it's not just a clean-cut image that attracts marketers; it's the complete package. Athletes must realize that sports is a business. Potentially, their endorsement deals can be more valuable than their salaries. One way to promote an athlete's visibility is through television commercials, since the focus is not on the team, but on the athlete.

Some of the more famous sports fashion images – examples of flamboyant, stylish, eminently recognizable sports figures – come from the '70s. Walt "Clyde" Frazier is noted for the way he dressed. Former Pittsburgh Steeler John "Frenchy" Fuqua knew how to make a statement. He once had a pair of clogs with clear heels occupied by live, swimming goldfish. Nowadays, we realize we are living in a society that is largely based on how we dress and what we look like. Keeping that in mind, image development and preparation can be profitable. An agent can take an athlete and market him or her outside the sports arena. Look for companies that may be looking for a certain type of athlete. Athletes have to ask themselves: "How do I perceive myself? How do I want others to perceive me?" This can play a major role down the road. The media can be an athlete's best friend or his worst enemy. Image is essential. There are three images involved when it comes to sports marketing: the image of the company, the image of the athlete, and the image to be promoted. Putting these together is challenging.

Marketers look for athletes who are top performers. For years Nike has centered ad campaigns around Michael Jordan, because Jordan is unequivocally the best basketball player, and Nike knows consumers will make a mental connection if they are shown that the best athletes wear Nike apparel. The same principle applies to Reebok's use of Shaquille O'Neal and Emmitt Smith in advertisements.

Companies also look for certain personality traits. How articulate is the athlete? How charismatic is the athlete? Does the athlete have a certain aura about him?

From the endorsee's standpoint, once the contract is signed, the promotion begins. Endorsement deals are profit-oriented. Once the contract is signed and the promotion increases sales, the endorsee becomes a higher-profile company, which leads to a new contract. However, if the company does not see a significant increase in business through the course of the deal, the company will not resign the athlete. Athletes have to realize the importance of on-the-court performance, image, and media preparation. All these factors affect athlete endorsement opportunities.

Advertisers want to be associated with athletes who are likable, recognizable, and credible – athletes who are well-spoken and interesting. If an athlete wants to take advantage of the endorsement dollar, he or she should interact with the media. There are firms that train athletes in the art of becoming "endorsement-friendly." Programs are designed to prepare athletes to capture the interest of corporations or sponsors.

There is nothing worse than seeing an athlete with poor communication skills being interviewed before millions. Companies look for athletes who are articulate, who have positive personal images, and who are knowledgeable about what they do. There are many athletes who do not get endorsements because they do not have a marketable image.

While college athletes are not allowed to accept any money from product endorsements, shoe manufacturers have become wise to the growing importance, popularity, and impact of college sports. Companies now approach college athletic programs and coaches to provide uniforms and equipment for the teams. A manufacturer might pay a coach, for instance, to become the exclusive provider of shoes for a high-profile college team, turning college stars into unpaid endorsers. When the college stars graduate or leave school early to turn pro, the shoe company is there to offer them million-dollar endorsement contracts that will make them immediately rich, even though the athletes' actual salaries may be limited early in their careers due to salary cap restrictions.

Getting the Right Athlete to Endorse Your Product

What a product or service provider should do before signing an athlete to an endorsement contract:

- A background investigation is necessary to find out about the character of an athlete. The athlete should be given ample time to test the product and should be encouraged to take notes or respond in writing about how he or she feels about the product. Interview the athlete in person about the product. The bottom line: Can a business partnership work out for both parties?

Do not sign an athlete who is not willing to give 100%

- When an athlete signs his name on the dotted line, a partnership is formed. If the athlete does not want to follow through with necessary stipulations of the contract, the deal should not be consummated. Such an endorser will not have his heart in the campaign and will not be able to promote the product or service in a positive, professional manner.

Example of a bad endorsement deal:

- An investment company may have an athlete endorse its financial planning services, although the company is aware the athlete has no intention of personally following its financial planning advice. The company feels because the athlete is in the forefront, it will be a good deal for them. A year later, the athlete is bankrupt and the investment company withdraws the endorsement deal – not a good way to attract new customers.

- It is very important for endorsees to take responsibility and check the background and character of athletes who they recruit to endorse their products or services. In many cases, the endorsee may have worked extremely hard to create the product or service. Sports Services of America™ maintains as much of this information on file as possible and has sources to obtain certain background and character information.

What is the responsibility of the athlete to the endorsee?

- As a business partner, the athlete should live up to all of the obligations and terms of his or her contract. If the athlete and the endorsee agree that the athlete should not engage in certain activities because it would be frowned upon by consumers, the athlete should honor the request. Conduct on and off the court must be consistent, because an athlete's image is associated with the product. Once the contract is signed and money changes hands, the athlete should follow the terms and stipulations of the contract.

What does signing an endorsement contract mean to an athlete?

- When an athlete signs his name on the dotted line the partnership begins. If the product does not perform, it hurts the credibility of the athlete. If the athlete does not perform, it hurts the credibility of the product. The athlete is stamping his seal of approval on the product or service.

What should an athlete do before endorsing a product or service?

- If the endorsement deal is a product or service, the athlete should use the product for a period of time to become familiar and confident with it. He should put the product through a series of tests and make a report or take notes, then relay his findings to his future business partner – the endorsee. The athlete should believe in the product and support all the good that the product can do for consumers.

- An athlete's full cooperation is necessary. The more the athlete supports the idea of being in business with you, the stronger his stamp of approval will be. Through this association, both parties can benefit each other.

A look at LDDS WorldCom

LDDS WorldCom is relatively new to the athlete endorsement field. By signing Michael Jordan, LDDS WorldCom got the #1 endorser in the world. It began with TV commercials that featured Jordan calling households and trying to introduce LDDS to the public. The people who answered sound dumbfounded and hang up. In the meantime, Michael calls them from his car phone, exercise bike, and locker room, finding little success with this telemarketing approach to long distance.

LDDS' promotion included long-distance collector's cards featuring Michael Jordan. One of the promotional mailings was a life-size outline of Michael's hand. The affiliation with Michael Jordan gives LDDS an added boost in introducing itself to the competitive long distance market. The three main competitors in this market are AT&T, Sprint, and MCI. The slogan LDDS WorldCom uses to go along with Michael Jordan's endorsement is "Service that's one-on-one."

The following is an interview I conducted with Gail Blount, manager of advertising sales at LDDS WorldCom.

Q: What is the relationship between athlete and product?

A: We look at two things. First, we want to know if the athlete would use our service. The second thing is 'Does the athlete's personal attributes match our corporate 'personality"?'

Q: What criteria do you use for signing an athlete to an endorsement contract?

A: We are interested in three things:

1. What degree of recognition does this athlete have with the general public?

2. Is the overall image favorable among the general public?

3. What is his degree of recognition by adult male decision-makers?

Currently, LDDS WorldCom sponsors selective events.

Q: Why do you sponsor a particular event?

A: We look at several things. First, what is the exceptional demographic the event is targeted to? Will it be cost-effective for us? The second thing we look at is the "rare ticket," which renders it an outstanding customer appreciation event. Finally, rolling out the new ad campaign. Could we deliver a new product to the consumer at this event?

Q: What is the relationship between product and event?

A: Demographics – the same individual that buys commercial or consumer long distance service is the one that attends or watches the event on TV.

Shaquille O'Neal is changing the relationship between athletes and business. He has several different endorsement avenues that he explores, and he has several business contracts. For instance, he is the owner of the "Shaq" logo and has an equity interest in almost every company he endorses. He also has starred in several movies: Blue Chips and Kazaam. O'Neal received a $4 million advance for "Kazaam." O'Neal also has a deal with William Neilson, Canada's largest candy company, allowing the company to market a line of "Shaq Snaqs" candies, including a "Mr. Big" chocolate bar. Amway even has a line of Shaq energy bars. O'Neal has also put out two rap albums.

It's not all fun and games for "Shaq." O'Neal once worked out a deal with Microsoft to promote its products. Microsoft was even running a promotion with Shaq and Bill Gates. When O'Neal defected to SportsLine USA, Microsoft's competitor, Microsoft wasted no time in hitting O'Neal where it hurts – the free-throw line. Microsoft produced a graphic portraying O'Neal shooting up brick after brick from the free-throw line, which was to illustrate Shaq's poor mechanics. The interactive graphic then illustrates the smoothness, grace, and simplicity of making free throws, using the example of Chicago Bull free-throw specialist Steve Kerr.

O'Neal has also closed a deal with the Universal Studios theme park in Orlando for "Shaq's Place," an area of the park due to open in two years that will feature a nightclub with a basketball theme. He received a $1.75 million advance. Shaq has his own World Wide Web site called "Shaq World," allowing users to see pictures of his home or the latest Pepsi ad. Shaquille O'Neal's marketing potential seems unlimited as his popularity grows. The Lakers agreed to shell out over $100 million to sign him during the free-agent frenzy of 1996. O'Neal will expand his endorsement portfolio in Hollywood as a Laker.

How powerful is Shaquille O'Neal's presence in Los Angeles? Coca-Cola was a sponsor for the Great Western Forum, home of the Lakers (NBA) and the Kings (NHL), but pulled its sponsorship after the Lakers acquired O'Neal, a Pepsi spokesman. A day later,

PepsiCo became the official sponsor of the Great Western Forum. Steve Koonin, a Coca-Cola spokesman, told a reporter, "The Lakers couldn't guarantee they would be able to protect our sponsorship from ambush marketing activities."

There is a constant debate about money and the entertainment value of sports. Athletes like O'Neal indulge in the entertainment field constantly and lucratively, and O'Neal is certainly not the only one. Wayman Tisdale released a jazz album, and Michael Jordan starred in a feature animated film for Warner Brothers. Athletes realize their job is evaluated based on their performance in battle, but more and more athletes are beginning to pursue other avenues. There is life after sports. Athletes are now artists and movie stars.

Just how many outside business ventures does Shaquille O'Neal have a hand in?

Lineup For O'Neal, Inc.

Shaquille O'Neal's move to Los Angeles may increase his endorsement resume. Here are his current corporate partners:

- All Star Café, restaurant
- Amway, vitamins and energy bar
- Cadbury Chocolate Canada, candy bars
- Interscope Communications, "Kazaam" motion picture

- Kenner Products, NBA toy figures

- NBA Entertainment, home videos

- NBA Properties, licensed products

- Neilson International, candy bars

- Pepsi-Cola Co., soft drink

- PepsiCo Restaurants International, global restaurant

- PPI Entertainment, home video

- Reading is Fundamental, charity

- Reebok International Ltd., apparel and shoes

- Score Board Inc., autographed memorabilia and trading cards

- SkyBox International Inc., trading cards

- Spalding Sports Worldwide, basketballs and backboards

- SportsLine, USA, World Wide Web online services

- Taco Bell, fast food

- Tiger Electronics Inc., hand-held games

- T.W.IsM Records, record label; his first CD, *Shaq Diesel*, sold more than 1 million copies (platinum); the second, *Shaq Fu: Da Return*, sold more than 500,000 (gold).

- Ultracom, international licensing

- Universal Studios Florida, public relations

- Warner Brothers, the movie "Steel"

Source: Management Plus

People may wonder why one athlete is more desirable than others. Michael Jordan's image is of winning and success. He is a hardworking, extremely talented athlete who has overcome adversity and still keeps his image intact. Michael Jordan is a professional who understands the nature of his business and who conducts himself with charm and class. Just when you think you've seen everything on the endorsement circuit, now comes a cologne for men: Michael Jordan. Jordan signed an endorsement with XEL, Inc. a subsidiary of Bijan fragrances. He now has his own signature fragrance.

The growth of athlete endorsements and joint ventures as sources of publicity and promotion for products should not be understated. Michael Jordan is probably the most recognizable athlete in the world. His name and face can be seen on anything from T-shirts to basketballs to video games to shoes and apparel. Jordan also endorses dozens of other consumer products, such as Gatorade, LDDS, McDonald's, Bijan, General Mills, and Pepsi. Together, his endorsement ventures bring in roughly $40 million.

Sports Figures and Endorsements

Carl Lewis, after failing to make the 1996 Olympics for the 100-yard dash, thanked Nike for its support. This is the kind of athlete a company should have as an endorser. He believes in the product and is more than willing to promote it. It also shows how a company can receive extra publicity by treating its endorsers well. Athletes may also receive incentives.

Troy Aikman of the Dallas Cowboys was fined $40,000 for wearing a pair of Adidas shoes in two preseason games. Adidas is not an official shoe of the National Football League. Players wearing shoes other than NFL-approved apparel must put tape over the logos. Aikman shoes flashed the Adidas logo, thereby costing him $20,000 per game in fines.

Consider the company Pro Player's move to shell out $2 million per year to rename Miami's Joe Robbie Stadium "Pro Player Park." The Pro Player spokesman, Miami Dolphin head coach Jimmy Johnson, receives around $300,000 a year from Pro Player. However, Johnson cannot wear Pro Player apparel on the sidelines. It is written in Johnson's contract with Pro Player that he must on all other occasions wear Pro Player, whenever he is around the media. The reason he cannot wear Pro Player on the sideline is that Pro Player is not NFL licensed. The agreement does not require Jimmy Johnson to wear a hat – thus, his unmovable hair will remain his trademark.

The Campbell Soup company signed Wayne Gretzky, who is known as "The Great One" and considered to be the best hockey player of all time. Campbell also worked with the NHL on a theme promotion for the Chunky Soup line. Gretzky will have his image on 50 million cans of Chunky Soup. Although this is the first time the image of an athlete will grace Campbell's Chunky Soup, it is not the first sports-themed promotion from Campbell. The company's other endeavors included contracts with NASCAR, Major League Baseball, and the NFL.

The Professional Golfers Association (PGA) multiplied its mere $55 million of prize money by a factor of three through endorsements. Payne Stewart, who finished sixth on the money prize list in 1993, parlayed that effort into a five-year, $8 million deal with Spalding Sporting Goods. He also has corporate deals for his shoes, balls, bags, hats, and clothes, bringing his total endorsement income to nearly $2 million, compared to the $146,000 he made in prize money on the tour in 1994. Corporations are banging on the door of players like Stewart because of television exposure. It offers a link between the country's nearly 25 million golfers and the hundreds of golf product manufacturers anxious to satisfy those duffers' desire to become better players.

There was a rumor that at one point in Michael Jordan's second year, after 17 games, he had broken his foot. The Bulls went into the postseason, and the team was opposed to Jordan playing too soon after his injury. The rumor was that Jordan, who had signed an endorsement deal with Nike, was urged by Nike to play in the postseason. Jordan played against the Celtics and had an all-time playoff game high of 63 points. Just a rumor.

Since 1990, the Kellogg Company has been a sponsor of NASCAR racing. In 1996, Kellogg's released a new cereal named Kellogg's Honey Crunch Corn Flakes, with the assistance of sponsored NASCAR #5 driver, Terry Labonte. Labonte's car will be designed to look like the packaging of the actual product. This marks the first time a product has been introduced using a NASCAR auto design. The product was also offered for free to fans at NASCAR races in order to promote the new cereal. In 1991, Kellogg's ran a promotion with NASCAR in which the company produced 25 limited-edition cereal boxes.

Tiger Woods had barely turned professional when he was given a five-year, $40 million endorsement from Nike and a five-year, $20 million endorsement from Acushnet Co., the parent company of Titleist and Cobra Golf. The deal with Acushnet commits Woods to the exclusive use of Titleist and Cobra products, which include Titleist golf balls, Titleist and Cobra Golf clubs, and a Titleist golf bag. This is significant. Tiger Woods has charisma, confidence, and is marketable as an African-American player in a predominantly white sport.

Can An Athlete Endorsement Affect Sales Of Products?

Nike is the number-one sports company in the world. When Michael Jordan temporarily retired in 1993, Nike's stock dropped. In March of 1994, when it was rumored that Jordan would return to the NBA following his brief baseball career, Nike stock went from 72 7/8 (March 1) to 76 1/4 (March 17). Some may say that's just a coincidence, while others point out that Jordan's presence has a definite, powerful influence on the business viability of endorsee companies and the NBA itself. The Chicago Bulls had won three consecutive NBA Championships. When Michael Jordan returned to the NBA for his first full season, the Chicago Bulls won their fourth championship in six years. Jordan won his eighth scoring title.

Current New York Yankee pitcher Dwight Gooden signed an endorsement contract with Regent Sports Corp. while he was playing for the Mets – a time when it looked like he'd have a brilliant career. The contract stipulated that Regent could have a glove model with Gooden's signature. Shortly thereafter, Gooden was suspended from baseball for drug use.

When this occurred, it was a shock to the company. A situation like this can blow over, but the problem is the negative press and how it affects the sales of the gloves with the athlete's signature, not to mention its effect on the athlete's image and that of the endorsee company. Regent had also signed Darryl Strawberry, who later admitted to a drug problem during the 1994 season. Regent was forced to disassociate itself from Strawberry because the negative publicity surrounding him affected the sales of his signature gloves.

When Dallas Cowboy wide receiver Michael Irvin ran into problems during the 1996 off-season, he was asked to return the $50,000 Toyota Land Cruiser he was driving. The Land Cruiser was given to him by Texas Toyota Dealers Association. Irvin agreed to return the Land Cruiser, and was also sued by the North Texas Toyota Dealers Association for $1.4 million in damages. The dealers were set for their spring ad campaign, which was to feature Irvin, but they were forced to scrap the project following Irvin's arrest. The association claimed that Irvin violated deceptive-trade laws when he signed an endorsement contract misrepresenting himself as a moral person. Irvin, along with a former teammate and two topless dancers, were allegedly in possession of marijuana, cocaine, and drug paraphernalia when they were found by police. The Toyota dealers association lawsuit seeks $1.2 million for lost sales and $200,000 in production costs.

Endorsing A Fallen Sports Celebrity

Many companies are scared to get involved with an athlete after he or she makes a mistake. This is where I, Kermit Pemberton, make a stand against my industry colleagues. What does an endorser get by endorsing a fallen member of the community? Here are some possible benefits:

1. The athlete must be ready to change his or her image and behaviors and agree to specified terms. Also, of course, the athlete must be willing to provide services to the endorser at a huge discount. Opportunistic endorsers should make sure the athlete's background is researched completely, and they should make sure the athlete is ready for change and capable of changing. If this is not possible, then it may be prohibitive of a contract.

• Business can receive high visibility at a fraction of the cost, especially if the athlete is winning/successful at the time.

• Endorsers can link community support-themed events with charitable events. Many times it is mandatory that the player appear and participate at community functions anyway.

- Athletes need love, support, and encouragement to help overcome some of their problems. Product and service manufacturers gain trust, sincerity, commitment, and loyalty with employees and customers, especially with those in the local community, who will be supportive of the fallen superstar if he or she pledges to reform.

When Nike became the sponsor for the Dallas Cowboys and decided to market replica jerseys, it chose for the jerseys the numbers of Emmitt Smith, Deion Sanders, Troy Aikman, Daryl Johnston, and Michael Irvin. When Irvin was suspended by the NFL and sentenced to four years of probation and 800 hours of community service, his replica jersey was no longer a hot item. Retailers report that sales of Michael Irvin jerseys have taken a downward plunge.

Negative publicity hurts both companies and athletes. Careful consideration is necessary. Companies are beginning to be more conservative and selective when signing athletes to endorsement deals.

The demands on the modern athlete go well beyond the field. The bottom line is that marketers will never stop using athletes to endorse products. Athletes who understand the value of their position can benefit the most by understanding sports as a business.

Ways Of Limiting Liability When Using A Celebrity Endorser

- Use more that one endorser; thus, the burden of maintaining credibility is balanced out and evenly distributed.

- Use the celebrity's likeness or image. Surveys have shown that over 77% of sports fans recognize the back of Michael Jordan's head.

- The use of retired athletes is another excellent way to reduce liability. By the time an athlete is retired, all of his old skeletons have been exposed. Fans often have a better trust factor because they have known the athlete for a long period of time.

Top Endorsement Earners

The following is a list of paid athletes detailing their endorsement contracts in 1995. Endorsements include traditional endorsement income, licensing royalties, exhibition, appearance fees, and money from celebrity-related activities, such as autograph signings and speeches.

Salaries/Winnings In Millions - (*Forbes* 1995)

Michael Jordan, age 32
    Endorsements: $40.0
    Salary/Winnings $3.9

Endorsements: Rayovac and Oakley Sunglasses, Nike, Wilson, McDonald's, Sara Lee (Hanes and Gatorade).

Shaquille O'Neal, age 23
    Endorsements: $17.0
    Salary/Winnings $4.9

O'Neal bridges athletics, endorsements, and entertainment. He has huge ongoing deals with Reebok and Pepsi.

Jack Nicklaus, age 55
    Endorsements: $14.5
    Salary/Winnings $0.6

Endorsements: Gulfstream, Lincoln-Mercury, Hartmarx, etc., aided by a new line of Jack Nicklaus accessories, ties and cufflinks.

Arnold Palmer, age 66
    Endorsements: $14.0
    Salary/Winnings $0.1

Endorsements: Cadillac, Rolex, and Pennzoil, among others. He has also entered into a lucrative licensing deal with the Hong Kong-based Chaifa Group for licensed apparel throughout mainland China.

Andre Agassi, age 25

| Endorsements: | $13.0 |
| Salary/Winnings | $3.0 |

The image-driven Agassi privately griped about being underpaid by Nike, almost jumping ship to Reebok. Fortunately for Nike, he agreed to accept a lucrative 10-year deal.

George Foreman, age 46

| Endorsements | $8.0 |
| Salary/Winnings | $10.0 |

Endorsements: Midas and many more

Greg Norman, age 40

| Endorsements | $8.0 |
| Salary/Winning | $1.7 |

Endorsements: Licensing arrangements, including his own line of golf sportswear from Reebok.

Pete Sampras, age 24

| Endorsements | $6.5 |
| Salary/Winnings | $4.7 |

Endorsements: Nike, Wilson rackets, and Movado watches. He pockets another $2 million or so playing in exhibitions and nabbing "appearance fees."

Deion Sanders, age 28

| Endorsements: | $6.0 |
| Salary/Winnings | $16.5 |

Endorsement deals with Nike, Pepsi, Sega, and Quality Inn

Wayne Gretzky, age 34

| Endorsements: | $6.0 |
| Salary/Winnings | $8.5 |

Endorsements: Coke, Campbell's Soup, L.A. Gear, and more.

Dale Earnhardt, age 44

| Endorsements: | $6.0 |

Salary/winnings: $2.4

Endorsements: Earnhardt makes over 100 public appearances a year. Fans now buy $50 million worth of Earnhardt souvenirs annually.

Michael Schumacher, age 26
    Endorsements: $5.0
    Salary/Winnings $10.0

Formula I racing is hugely popular throughout the world and is gaining steam in the United States.

Grant Hill, age 23
    Endorsements: $5.0
    Salary/Winnings $2.8
Endorsements: GMC Trucks, Kellogg's, McDonald's, Sprite, and Fila.

Michael Chang, age 23
    Endorsements: $5.0
    Salary/Winnings $2.6

Endorsements: Reebok, Prince rackets, and more.

Steffi Graf, age 26
    Endorsements: $5.0
    Salary/Winnings $2.5

Endorsements: Graf is the only woman to receive $5 million in endorsements in 1995. She has, however, been dropped by a longtime sponsor, General Motors. She has faced serious tax problems in her native country, Germany.

Boris Becker, age 28
    Endorsements: $4.5
    Salary/Winnings: $3.3

Very popular German tennis star.

Cal Ripken Jr., age 35
    Endorsements: $4.0
    Salary/Winnings: $6.3

Endorsements: Nike and more.

Charles Barkley, age 32
      Endorsements: $3.0
      Salary/Winnings: $4.1

Endorsements: Sir Charles is with Nike. Sports marketers believe that Phil Knight shells out big bucks to the charismatic Barkley, as much to keep him away from Reebok as to retain him at Nike.

Steve Young, age 34
      Endorsements $3.0
      Salary/Winnings $4.0

Endorsements: Advil, Pepsi, the Dairy Council, Wheaties, Sun Microsystems, and Nike

Evander Holyfield, age 33
      Endorsements $2.0
      Salary/Winnings: $11.0

"The Real Deal" came back to boxing competition after he was diagnosed with a heart condition. He is my favorite boxer.

Patrick Ewing, age 33
      Endorsements: $2.0
      Salary/Winnings: $7.5

Endorsements: He has partial ownership of Ewing Athletics.

Hakeem Olajuwon, age 32
      Endorsements: $2.0
      Salary/Winnings: $5.8

Endorsements: Taco Bell, Spalding sneakers, Visa, Compaq, Uncle Ben's, Mars, and the NBA itself, which pays him about $150,000 to be its "international ambassador."

David Robinson, age 30
      Endorsements: $1.7

| Salary/Winnings | $7.9 |

His contract each year ensures that he will be one of the two highest-paid players in his sport, based on average salary. (The NBA will not allow other players to sign similar deals.)

Ken Griffey Jr., age 26
| Endorsements: | $1.7 |
| Salary/Winnings: | $6.2 |

Endorsements: Nike, Nintendo, and more.

Dan Marino, age 34
| Endorsements: | $1.7 |
| Salary/Winnings | $4.5 |

Endorsements: Marino is a member of the Quarterback Club, an elite group that generates extra money by licensing jersey replicas and jackets.

Frank Thomas, age 27
| Endorsements: | $1.5 |
| Salary/Winnings: | $6.3 |

Endorsements: Frank Thomas owns a sports marketing company called Big Hurt Enterprises.

Mark Messier, age 34
| Endorsements: | $1.0 |
| Salary/Winnings: | $6.0 |

Endorsements: Mariah Entertainment (video game), L.A. Gear (street hockey), and Starter (apparel). Brother Paul and father Doug negotiate his hockey contracts, while kid sister Mary-Kay handles the off-ice deals.

Jerry Rice, age 33
| Endorsements: | $1.0 |
| Salary/Winnings: | $6.0 |

Endorsements include deals with teammate Steve Young. He single-handedly made the CNS "Breathe Right" nose apparatus famous during the 1995 Super Bowl.

Drew Bledsoe, age 23
        Endorsements: $0.7
        Salary/Winnings: $13.2

Regarded as a local hero before the season.

Barry Bonds, age 31
        Endorsements: $0.7
        Salary/Winnings: $6.8
Bonds is arguably the best player in baseball. However, what he calls "just being myself" has cost him in the endorsement department.

Michael Irvin, age 29
        Endorsements: $0.7
        Salary/Winnings: $6.2

Endorsements: Nike, Southwest Airlines, Nose Guard, and Dr Pepper. He also owns Playmaker Productions – the company that produces his local TV shows – and a clothing outfit called Masterpeace Ragz.

Riddick Bowe, age 28
        Endorsements: $0.2
        Salary/Winnings: $22.0

1995 brought three fights and three big paydays for the man some consider "the best heavyweight boxer in the world."

Mike Tyson, age 29
        Endorsements: $0.0
        Salary/Winnings: $40.0

Endorsements: none. Three million homes paid approximately $60 per household to watch Tyson demolish Peter McNeeley in 89 seconds – good for a $25 million payday for Tyson.

The 1996-1997 "Ten Most Wanted" Spokespersons

This list is based on estimated endorsement earnings from August 1996 through July 1997. It indicates the demand each athlete generates from potential endorsee companies. Figures were furnished by Sponsorship Research International, and dollar amounts do not include salary.

Note: There is not much change from the 1995 list that appeared in *Forbes*.

1) **Michael Jordan** – Estimated 1996-97 earnings: $38 million. Sponsors: *Nike, Rayovac, Gatorade, Sara Lee Corp. (Hanes, Ballpark Franks, Coach Leather), General Mills (Wheaties), Upper Deck and Upper Deck Authenticated, Warner Brothers movie "Space Jam" (11/96 release), Oakley Sunglasses, Wilson (signature basketballs, watches, golf, baseball equipment), NBA Entertainment/CBS-Fox Home Videos, Bijan, Chicago Chevyland, Jordan's Restaurant, MJ Golf.*

2) **Shaquille O'Neal** – Estimated 1996-97 earnings: $23 million. Sponsors: *Reebok, Taco Bell (U.S.), KFC and Pizza Hut (internationally), Pepsi, Electronic Arts, Universal Studios-Orlando (Shaq's Place), SkyBox Classic Games, TWiSM Records, TWiSM Apparel, Tiger Electronics, Spalding (signature basketballs, equipment), Scoreboard, Interscope Entertainment, Tsumara Intl. (kids' toiletries), Kenner, All-Star Café, Amway, Neilson Intl., Warner Bros. (films), SportsLine (Shaq World Wide Web site).*

3) **Arnold Palmer** – Estimated 1996-97 earnings: $16 million. Sponsors: *Cadillac, Textron, Arnold Palmer Golf Co., Federated Dept. Stores, The Golf Channel, Lexington Furniture, Lofts Seed Co., 84 Lumber, Rayovac,*

PNC (Pittsburgh National Bank), Pennzoil, Office Depot, GTE, DP Fitness Equipment, Rolex, and more.

4) **Andre Agassi** – Estimated 1996-97 earnings: $15.8 million. Sponsors: Nike, Pepsi, Canon, Head (racquets), Swiss Army Watch, All Star Café, and more. (Agassi's Nike deal is worth around $10 million.)

5) **Jack Nicklaus** – Estimated 1996-97 earnings: $14.3 million. Sponsors: Lincoln-Mercury, Hartmarx, Rolex, Accolade, Rockport, Maxfli, Gulfstream Aerospace, Republic Home Video, Trans Apparel Group, EZ-GO Textron, Golf Magazine, Nicklaus Golf Equipment, and more. Nicklaus has also licensed the use of his name for clothing and accessories.

6) **Grant Hill** – Estimated 1996-97 earnings: $14 million. Sponsors: GMC Trucks, Fila, Kellogg, McDonald's, Coca-Cola (Sprite), Wilson, Ohio Art, and other licensing deals.

7) **Joe Montana** – Estimated 1996-97 earnings: $12 million. Sponsors: Upper Deck Authenticated, LCI International, Coors, SportsLine, PacificHealth laboratories (workout supplement), Dayton Hudson, Franklin Templeton, Hanes, Fitness Quest, L.A. Gear, Opus (publishing), Chip Ganassi/Target Racing, and more.

8) **Wayne Gretzky** – Estimated 1996-97 earnings: $8.75 million. Sponsors: L.A. Gear, Upper Deck, Upper Deck Authenticated, All-Star Café, Wayne Gretzky's Roller Hockey Centers, Atari Interactive Video, Ultra Wheels, Coca-Cola, Zurich Insurance, Easton, Campbell's Soup, Mariah Entertainment, and CCM (ice hockey skates).

9) **Deion Sanders** – Estimated 1996-97 earnings: $6 million. Sponsors: Nike, Pepsi, Sega, Visa, Sports Specialties (headwear), Burmax (bandannas), and more.

10) **Hakeem Olajuwon** – Estimated 1996-97 earnings: $5 million. Sponsors: Taco Bell, Spalding, NBA Entertainment and Properties, Compaq, Oshman's Sporting Goods, Visa, Frito-Lay, AT&T, Bill Heard Chevrolet (Houston), Kellogg, Uncle Ben's Rice, Minolta, Score Board, and Rochester Big and Tall

Times are changing. There are many new products and services that companies want to promote through sports. This trend has proven to have great financial rewards. The visibility of athletes has become more prevalent in the last decade. The pressure on athletes is enormous due to media exposure, expectations, and high salaries. However, endorsement opportunities stretch beyond the sports arena. Businesses that in the past traditionally did not use athletes to endorse their products are now branching off into the sports world. This trend will continue to increase.

Types of Endorsements

Many different deals can be worked out. Athletes can work on a percentage basis. Products can be exchanged for endorsements, or products and services can be exchanged for public exposure. Both sides have to agree, and it should be specified what exactly each party will be receiving.

Merchandise agreement: A merchandise agreement is very similar to an endorsement agreement. The main difference is that the athlete's compensation is given in the form of merchandise.

Licensing: There is a slight difference between a license agreement and an endorsement agreement. All endorsement agreements are promotional in nature, while in a license agreement an athlete, team, or other sports organization grants the rights to use a name, image, logo, or likeness.

Media Special: This type of endorsement can include any kind of media in which the athlete is seen or heard endorsing a product. One example would be if an athlete is being interviewed and says, "I would like to thank Nike for its support." Another may be the athlete appearing on the cover of Sports Illustrated with a Reebok logo hat. These are examples of Media Special endorsements.

Performance-Based Endorsements (Performance Bonus)

The following chart is an example of the terms of a contract an athlete might receive with a glove manufacturer using his signature on the product:

Errors*	Bonus
0	$100,000
5	$90,000
10	$30,000
15	$10,000
20	$7,500
25 or more	$5,000

* In baseball, errors are a statistical mark given by official scorekeepers when a fielder makes a mistake that negatively impacts his team (e.g. allows a runner to reach a base, allows a run to score, etc.)

The purpose of these types of contracts is to protect the product manufacturer or service provider from endorsing an athlete who does not live up to the image expected of him. These contracts represent a sliding scale based on athlete performance. Consider a situation in which a baseball player who endorses your hot dogs only hits .250. He is paid $10,000 as a flat rate, but if he hits over .250, he receives $100 for each batting percentage point. The contract pays the athlete for performance on a sliding scale. This contract can cover anything from strikeouts to home runs.

Performance Bonus Schedule For
American Group Or National Group League

Accomplishment	Bonus
James Trophy Award Winner	$5,000
Marmalades Relief Pitcher of the Year	$10,000
or	
Thirty or more saves	$5,000
Leader in games won	$15,000
If not leader in games won:	N/A
If endorser has 20 or more wins:	$10,000
If endorser has 15 to 19 wins:	$6,500
Note: Awards are not cumulative	Yes
Leader in innings pitched	$10,000
Leader in games pitched	N/A
Pitches complete-game no-hitter	$5,000
Member of mid-year All-Star team	$7,500
Most Valuable Player in All-Star Game	$4,000
Most Valuable Player in World Series	$5,000
Most Valuable Player in playoffs	N/A
Gold Glove winner	N/A

TEAM SPORTS

ENDORSEMENT AGREEMENT

STANDARD TERMS

A. Endorser Name and Address:

> c/o Kermit Pemberton
>
> Sports Services of America™
>
> Marina Del Rey, CA 90292

B. Effective date of Agreement:	6/18/96
C. Term:	6/18/96-6/18/98 (2 years)
D. Territory:	U.S.
E. Brand:	Fun Sporting Goods Co.
F. Endorsed Products:	fielder's gloves
G. Appearance:	2 @ $5,000 (optional)
H. Signature Product Right:	N/A
I. Percentage Royalty on Signature Products:	3%
J. Guaranteed Minimum Compensation:	N/A
K. Equipment to be supplied by Fun to Endorser:	For each contract year during which endorser is on the active roster of a Major Group baseball team, Fun agrees to provide endorser with $10,000 worth of Fun retail merchandise (based on catalog cost).
L. Renewal Option Period:	None
M. Other Supplemental Provisions to the Standard Terms:	
N. Signatures:	This agreement between Fun Sporting Goods Co. and

endorser, consists of the following incorporated parts: the standard terms, this supplement, and (if checked) (X) the performance bonus.

Schedule -- and is executed this ___ day of _____, 1997

Fun Sporting Goods Co.   ENDORSER

By: _____   By: _____

Title: _____   Social Security No:

                                          _____

                                          (If endorser is a corporation)

                                          Personal Guarantee:

                                          Printed Name of Guarantor:

                                          Federal Tax ID No:

Chapter 6

Athlete Marketing

PUBLIC SPEAKING, PUBLIC RELATIONS, BOOK PUBLISHING

CAMPS, TOURNAMENTS, FAN CLUBS, FOUNDATIONS, ONE-DAY SEMINARS

An athlete or sports celebrity has opportunities to earn money in public speaking. For an athlete to take advantage of this aspect of the industry, he/she should prepare. The average length of an athletic career is extremely limited, but with increased exposure for sports and athletes, a public speaking career can last a lifetime. Prior to entering into this field, these are a few things an athlete or sports celebrity should work on: public speaking, presentation, and speechwriting/reading (although a speech writer could be hired). It may also be necessary to hire a speech therapist and an image consultant. Companies that consider contracting with an athlete for speaking engagements may require a videotape of the athlete's overall presentation. Learning to speak publicly is a great asset and may also lead into a career as a TV or radio sportscaster.

Sports Celebrity Motivational Speakers And The Lucrative World Of Public Speaking

An athlete is paid to make a speech to a group, association, meeting, or assembly. The most common topics generally revolve around motivation. Topics may include self-development, customer service, teamwork, or sales.

An athlete should join a full-service speakers bureau such as Sports Services of America™. There are also national and local trade associations of speakers. A speakers bureau markets speakers to meeting planners, trade associations, advertising agencies, and public relations firms. If an athlete is seriously interested in earning an income through public speaking, he should have a press kit and a video or audio tape sample of himself speaking. This is standard procedure on the public speaking circuit and is a great advantage – most clients will request a tape.

An agent represents speakers. Usually a speaker has an exclusive agreement with one agent, sometimes guaranteeing the number of speaking engagements per year. Such guarantees are usually only agreed to by celebrity speakers. Agents are in charge of publicity and promotion for their client, and also work with bureau brokers to plan speaking arrangement dates.

Public speaking is an excellent way for an athlete to earn additional income during his sports career and to continue to make a living when his sports career ends. There are companies that specialize in coaching athletes on appearance and speaking skills.

Meeting planners and other executives who book sports speakers contend that a well-delivered motivational talk to a sales force inspires short-term results. The kick tends to wear off, though, so another shot of concentrated competitive spirit is required before long. This has led to a market for hot-ticket, high-profile coaches and athletes who work the corporate-inspiration circuit. Earnings sometimes exceed $20,000 per speech, and the area is growing rapidly. Speaking engagements with sports figures represent a large percentage of the U.S. meeting-and-convention industry, which brings in an estimated $75 billion annually.

The following are some sports celebrity speakers who lead the way:

For $20,000 and a first-class plane ticket, Coach Rick Pitino ("America's Most Energetic Motivational Speaker") of the Kentucky Wildcats will reveal his secrets of managing and motivating a winning team. Lecture agencies, which collect 20% of Pitino's speaking fees, call him the "Manager of the '90s" and claim, "He'll energize your team." Most of the time, Pitino speaks to senior managers, but he handles speeches differently depending on his audience. For example, if he is talking to upper management, he talks to them as if they were coaches. When he talks to salespeople, he alters his speech and speaks to them as recruits.

Pitino's inspirational speeches are laden with key elements that all listeners will remember. He uses a study aid – the acronym "TEAM" – to guide his talks. For instance, the "A" in TEAM stands for attitude, and he illustrates this by telling stories of the attitude problems he encountered with the Knicks between 1985 and 1987. By using this approach, Pitino has learned to captivate his audience.

Other sports celebrity speakers also use study aids to guide their speeches, and also to help audiences absorb the message. Mike Ditka, the former coach of the Chicago Bears who is now a broadcaster, uses the code word "ACE," which stands for "Attitude, Character, and Enthusiasm," to bring in $2 million a year on the lecture circuit. Lou Holtz, former head coach of Notre Dame football, prefers "WIN," for "What's Important Now." Pat Riley, reputed to be one of the most-requested sports speakers in the country, prefers an amalgam of "rules," including the "Rule of the Rebirth, Rule of the Heart, and Rule for the Triumph."

The following is a list of sports celebrities and their public speaking fees:

Name	Fee	Notes
Lou Holtz	$25,000	
Dan Jansen	$20,000	
Rick Pitino	$20,000	
Mike Ditka	$20,000	
Dick Vitale	$18,000	
Bruce Jenner	$13,500	
Neil Smith	$10,000	
Derrick Thomas	$10,000	
Tommy Lasorda	$12,500	
Terry Bradshaw	$10,000	
Steve Garvey	$8,500	
Joe Morris	$5,000	
Jerry Kramer	$5,000	One of the first speakers on the business talk circuit to lean on tales about his late coach, Vince Lombardi.
Vince Lombardi Jr.	$3,500	Looks like his father, sounds like him, and even speaks him.

Currently, 400 agencies jockey to book the 300 most capable sports speakers. In order to gain a competitive edge in this field of agencies, superior service must be provided. When meeting planners or executives call, find out what type of speech they desire and inquire about budget, location, and time. After determining their preferences, fax a list of available speakers.

There is enormous potential in public speaking. Make deals that allow you to capitalize on fees. Understand that 20% to 33% of the quoted fees go to the agent. Hard work instills loyalty between you and the speaker. Busy speakers sometimes opt for an exclusive arrangement. In an exclusive arrangement, the agent absorbs promotional costs and manages the paperwork. Speaker bureaus also arrange for lessons with speaking coaches and make valuable suggestions on delivery and style. However, most speakers remain independent.

The average sports celebrity earns $3,500 to $7,500 for a speaking engagement. Superstar sports celebrities can receive $7,500 to $25,000. Athletes are generally paid to appear for no more than two hours. In that time span, they speak, shake hands, take pictures, and sign autographs.

Autograph Signings

An athlete is paid a set amount of money for signing his name to sports-related items. The items signed by the athlete become labeled "signed sports memorabilia." The value of an autograph is based on the popularity of the athlete, along with the supply and demand of his or her signature. Although an athlete's signature may not be worth anything when it is given, it can very well triple in value based on the athlete's future performance and popularity.

Autographs and autographed paraphernalia account for an enormous business. Similar to trading cards, autographs have a book value depending on the athlete, rarity, and item. However, be cautious about what you buy. The FBI recently released a report estimating that 70% of all autographs are forged. Certificates of Authenticity are rendered valueless. Unless they see the athlete sign the item, collectors are urged not to buy.

Major League Baseball revenue in 1990 totaled over $1.5 billion, and the revenue had increased every year since 1986. Roughly 1,500 MLB products were manufactured by over 300 licensees. The categories included apparel, headgear, sporting goods, novelties, gifts, toys and games, school supplies, trading cards, and other collectibles.

The following are questions posed to a long-time friend, autograph collector Glen Lentz of Starmount, at the 1996 National Collector Show.

Q   Do you agree with the FBI that over 70% of autographs are phony?

A   I agree with the FBI. It may be more than 70%. It's bad for honest collectors like myself.

Q   Glen, what can you do to ensure that you are purchasing real autographs?

A   Hope that you are buying from an honest person. The best way is to actually see the person signing the picture in person. I wish I could tell you more, but everyone is selling [forgeries] – even some of the bigger companies out there. I really wish I could tell you more.

Q   What is the most interesting piece you've sold this month?

A   A Rocky Marciano vs. Jersey Joe Walcott reprint of the original poster with an unused ticket of the fight. It had two 8x10 photos originally signed by each fighter. The poster sold for $2,500.

Q   Why did the gentleman buy the picture of the two boxers?

A   He liked the old boxing legacy and he felt he was a part of that era. He thought those were real tough fighters in those days. He owns a macadamia nut farm in Hawaii, and that's a tough way to make a living. So I think he loved the print because he related to the toughness of both fighters.

Many times an athlete can charge per signature based on the item he is signing. The athlete is not directly paid by the individual receiving the autograph. The person getting the autographed article pays the promoter to purchase the signature. An example of charges would be $30 a signature on jerseys, $20 on balls, and $10 on photos.

PRICES FOR SIGNING SPECIFIED ITEMS AT 1996 NATIONAL COLLECTOR'S SHOW

Kareem Abdul-Jabbar
Balls $60
Flats $45
Shoes/Odd $50
Jerseys $75

Wilt Chamberlain
Balls $90
Flats $60
Oddsize $75
Jerseys $120

Reggie Jackson
Balls/Flats $40
Jersey/Odds $100
Bats $175

Johnny Unitas
Flats $50
Mini Helmets/Balls $70
Jersey/Helmets $80
Oddsize 16 x 20 $55

Muhammad Ali
Flats $90
Robes $100
Oddsize $100
Gloves $120

Whitey Ford
Jerseys/Bats $60
Oddsize $60
Posters over $60
Balls/Bats $25

Harmon Killebrew
Bats/Jersey $60
Oddsize $60
Balls/Flats $25

Jim Brown
Balls/Flats $25
Oddsize $25
Jersey $35
Helmet $35

Steve Garvey
Jersey/Bats $50
Balls/Flats $17

Sandy Koufax
Balls/Flats $60
Jerseys/Oddsize $80

Ronnie Lott
Flats $30
Balls $50
Jersey/Bats $60
Oddsize $65

Duke Snider
Balls/Flats $26
Bats/Jersey $63
Oddsize/
Willie-Mickey-Duke Items $63

Dave Winfield
Balls/Flats $40
Bats/Jersey
Oddsize $65

Dennis Rodman
Balls $65
Flats $45
Jerseys $90
Oddsize 16x20 $60

Tom Seaver
Balls/Flats $35
Jerseys/Bats $65
Oddsize $65

Rollie Fingers
8x10 Photo $14.50
Balls $16.50
16x20 Photo $50
Bat/Oddsize $26.50

Pee Wee Reese
Balls/Flats $45
Mini-Balls $45
Hats/Gloves $60
Equipment $60
Jersey/Bats $85
Oddsize $85

Book Publishing

Books about athletes have always captured the imagination of the public. A biography about an athlete is a good vehicle through which an athlete can describe himself off the field of battle. Book signings and book tours take place on the talk show circuit. This is potentially a lucrative field for an athlete, and I recommend it to athletes to enhance their images and increase visibility. A book is a good way to do this.

Dennis Rodman – dressed in a silver halter top, black leather pants, and a hot pink and black feather boa with matching silver hair and nails – appeared before a crowd of 10,000 people in Chicago for his first book signing in the city. He signed 1,500 books and that was merely the beginning. Rodman's book, *Bad As I Wanna Be*, became number one on the nonfiction list. In the book's first week, the publisher went back to press six times, producing a total of 650,000 books.

Dennis Rodman did something so unusual that it captured a lot of attention. In the past couple of years, Rodman has been one of the most controversial athletes. His determination on the court is undeniable. In this atmosphere, *controversy sells*. Rodman's ingenious self-promotion generated publicity and press. He was highlighted in magazines ranging from *Sports Illustrated* to *Playboy*. He has been on numerous talk shows and signed a contract with MTV to host 20 episodes of his own show. Rodman's visibility increased beyond the sports scene. His face was on everything from billboards to bookstores. His marketing image is enhanced by his unpredictable antics on and off the court.

In most cases, the athlete does not write his book. He works with a ghostwriter, generally a sports writer or a newspaper sports reporter. While marketing the book, an athlete's publicist may require him or her to appearance on television programs, talk shows, and radio shows. A publicist creates press release clippings and contacts schools, libraries, and just about anything else imaginable to draw attention and increase visibility.

Self-publishers can work through distributors. Distributors and retail book stores usually deduct 50-60% of the retail price of the book.

An athlete may also hire a literary agent to represent and market his book. Many literary agents already have established relationships with the distributors. The advantage of this arrangement is that an established literary agent will know the business inside and out. A good agent will also know the tricks of the trade, whereas an inexperienced agent may not have this expertise.

The athlete may also set up a contract with a publishing house to write, edit, distribute, and market the book. When a manuscript is purchased by a major publisher and printed, the author usually receives royalties of 10% to 25% for each copy sold, depending on the contract. He may even receive an advance against royalties, which is a lump-sum payment based on the estimated earnings from sales of the book.

Big Dollars In Self-Publishing

If a book sold one million copies at $22 a book, that's $22 million. The distributor/retailer will take 50% of the retail price of the book, which leaves $11 million. Of that $11 million, the athlete can pay for the production of the book and the ghostwriter of the book. A ghostwriter's percentage can vary depending on the arrangement. The ghostwriter may be paid a percentage or flat fee. A book may cost up to $2.50 to print a paperback, or up to $5.50 for a hard-cover copy. Profit for the athlete is largely based on sales figures. Of the total of $22 million, the athlete would take home around $3-6 million.

Sports Celebrity Camps

Camps usually provide lodging, food, and merchandise. The size and price of the camp usually depends on the popularity of the athlete. If set up properly, the return on such camps is highly profitable. For a camp to be successful, there has to be organization, reputation, and credibility. Often sports celebrities can enhance the enrollment in a camp.

Summer camps are becoming more and more popular. In 1995, over five million young people attended day and resident summer camps, up from four million in the mid-1980s. These camps provide a high potential for profit. The average camp costs $450 per child, with an average attendance of 200. A camp can be sponsored. In order to solicit sponsors for camps, one needs a proposal that highlights the benefits of sponsorship. (For examples of sponsorship proposals, see the Sponsorship section.) Camps can be educational and exciting to attend, giving young fans the opportunity to receive instruction from coaches and players.

The majority of sports camps are held on college campuses across the country. Camps can range from Lacrosse at Princeton to basketball at UCLA. Colleges also tend to hold more than one camp at a time. College coaches run general sports camps. Athletes also run sports camps, such as Emmitt Smith's football camp or Jim Brown's football camp.

If the athlete is in a team sport, the athlete is usually more popular in the home town of the team in which he or she plays. If it's an individual sport, the camp may be centrally located. If the athlete is not especially popular, he or she may hold the camp at a well-known facility such as the Pauley Pavilion on the UCLA campus. This is a great facility for a basketball camp. Athletes also endorse camps and visit while the camp is in session. This usually occurs with a hometown hero or a national celebrity athlete. Athlete camps tend to draw more attention mainly because they give kids an opportunity to meet athletes who participate in a given sport.

Instructional camps are the most common form of sports-oriented camps, and the number of instructional camps is increasing every year. Instructional camps are usually run by coaches or players who teach kids the fundamentals of the sport. Some camps that don't have athlete guests try to arrange an athlete appearance by speaking with colleges or the public-relations departments of professional teams. Keep in mind that this can be a regional athlete. If the camp is for charity, sometimes special appearances can be arranged.

Sponsorship For Camps

The most important task for creating a financially successful camp is finding a sponsor (*see production of a special event for proposal*). Finding a title sponsor helps pay for some expenses in exchange for name recognition or donation of merchandise. If it's a basketball camp, Nike, Adidas, or Reebok may donate uniforms and footwear bearing the company logo. (*Refer to Sponsorship section.*)

Sponsorship money reduces overhead and helps to make a camp financially successful. Finding a sponsor will require a proposal, including a detailed advertising/marketing budget. Certain community institutions such as banks participate in local events. This gives them promotional advantages and illustrates a commitment to the community. Sponsoring banks receive CRA (Community Reinvestment Act) credit. The CRA has guidelines and suggestions that banks follow by setting goals for themselves to invest in the community. For instance, banks will lend money to a local charity or a larger one such as Habitat for Humanity, or they will sponsor an event such as the Juvenile Diabetes Walk for the Cure.

The best place to advertise a sports camp

The Sports section of the local newspaper is a good and reasonable place to advertise for camps. One may also advertise through national sport trade magazines, sport trade associations, and fliers at local gyms, courts, and courses. All camps publish brochures that include services, housing, cost, instructional development, objectives, and itinerary.

Generally there are two types of camps: day camp and overnight camp. The following is an example of a day camp:

<u>Kermit Pemberton's Golf Camp</u>

All sessions are during the day. Registration starts 8:30 a.m. and camp concludes at 3:00 p.m. A confirmation letter will be sent to confirm receipt of payment and to give directions.

What to bring:

- *Lunch*
- *Comfortable golf attire – golf shoes, etc.*
- *Professional attitude*
- *Extra currency for camp store and refreshment stand*

Camp highlights

- *Free camp golf balls*
- *Camp picture*
- *Special guest speakers*
- *Special shooting contests*
- *Free camp T-shirt*
- *Awards ceremonies*
- *Practice-round play*
- *Written player evaluation*

Camp Dates and Location:
Municipal University Golf Course
June 18 through June 22
Cost: $295.00
Sponsors: Hot Hand Deodorant, Fuel Bar, Penny Soda
         Co.

____ $1,000: Company name on our campers' T-shirts, Name on our banner, customized prize bag.

____ $500 Name on campers' T-shirts.

SAMPLE INFORMED CONSENT RELEASE
AUTHORIZATION FOR EMERGENCY TREATMENT

"I, the undersigned, as the parent or legal guardian of the child listed on this application, grant permission for my son/daughter to participate in the Kermit Pemberton Golf Camp, and hereby assume full responsibility for all risk of injury or losses that may result from my son's/daughter's participation in this activity. I hereby agree to release and discharge Kermit Pemberton and his officers, agents, and employees from responsibility, and waive any and all claims and demands whatsoever which the undersigned and any of them or any third person and their representatives or any persons acting on their behalf may have against said party or his officers, agents, or employees by reason of any loss or destruction of any property, accident, illness, injury, or death of any person or persons resulting directly or indirectly from my son's/daughter's participation in the aforementioned program, excepting that the above provisions shall not be applicable to injury, death, damage, or loss of property arising out the sole negligent acts or omissions of Kermit Pemberton or his officers, agents, or employees. The terms of this release shall serve as a release and assumption of risk for my son/daughter, heirs, executors, and administrators and for all of my family members."

"I understand that I am required to maintain and carry accident and medical insurance coverage for the child listed on this application and verify that the coverage information attached here is accurate and true."

"In the case of an emergency and if I cannot be reached, I hereby authorize the staff of the Kermit Pemberton Golf Camp to obtain whatever medical treatment they deem necessary for the welfare of my child listed on this application. I further understand and agree that I will be financially responsible for all charges and fees incurred in the rendering of said emergency treatment, regardless of whether or not my medical insurance would cover such charges and fees."

Informed Consent Release - page 2

"Having read and understood, and being in agreement with this release, I have signed and dated this application in the space provided below."

PLEASE READ INFORMED CONSENT AND RELEASE AUTHORIZATION.

I have read and understood, and I agree with the informed Consent and Release Authorization outlined in this brochure as it relates to my son or daughter.

Parent or Guardian Signature _____

Insurance Co. _____

Policy No. _____

Tournaments

A tournament is an organized competition in which the winners receive prizes.

Tournaments are usually good for the sponsors, because they receive a considerable amount of exposure. Look for companies that would be willing to donate prizes, which will allow you to avoid the expense of financing the prizes, and the company will receive publicity. To operate a tournament after prizes and advertising costs, the chance of profit is fair without corporate support.

Summer tournaments that run from June through July provide an important showcase for players. If it's a basketball tournament, it gives coaches the opportunity to scout top high school seniors at one venue instead of having to go from high school to high school.

From a marketing standpoint, these tournaments provide an excellent showcase for companies to promote products.

Shoe companies create tournaments and waive fees for top players to encourage them to attend. This practice ensures a higher-profile tournament, which helps to attract less well-known players who pay a fee to compete. Tournament organizers sometimes offer free shoes, sporting equipment, and athletic wear for participants. These perks are an effort to lure top players to the tournaments. In addition to being walking advertisements for the athletic wear companies, the athletes provide feedback about the products, and this feedback is used to formulate marketing strategies.

FAN CLUBS

A fan club is a private membership organization based on admiration of an athlete. The fans are able to receive special membership privileges, which may include the following:

- *Membership cards*
- *T-shirts*
- *Hats*
- *Autograph memorabilia*
- *Special appearances*
- *Chats on the Internet with the athlete*

- *Letters from the athlete*

- *Special discounts*

- *Annual meetings*

A fan club is a great way for an athlete to communicate with his fans and improve his relationship with the community. The profit is fairly small in most cases, unless there is a special event planned at the end of the sports season. An example of a special event is an outing in which fan club members play golf with a celebrity athlete or attend a dinner or retreat.

Sample fan club order form
Big "Ed" Thomas FOOTBALL FAN CLUB
Marketed by Sports Services of America™
I hereby apply for membership in the Big "Ed" Thomas Fan Club. I understand that the $29.95 membership fee is good for one year. In return, I will receive the following Big "Ed" Thomas Fan club package (postage included):
Big "Ed" Thomas T-shirt
Autographed photo
Fan club membership card
Surprise gift
Name_____
Address_____
City _____ State _____
Zip_____
Phone_____
Date of Birth_____
T-shirt size   S   M   L   XL   XXL
For more information on Big "Ed" Thomas Summer Youth Basketball Camps or Big "Ed" Thomas Fan Club Merchandise
please call: (310) 821-4490
please FAX: (310) 821-0522
Mail this form along with check or money order for $29.95 (postage and handling included) to:
The Big "Ed" Fan Club
333 Washington Blvd. #360

Marina Del Rey, CA 90292
Please allow 4 to 6 weeks for processing and delivery

The activities, such as a golf tournament, usually overlap into an athlete's foundation and can be used to raise money for a charitable cause. Fan club members receive a discounted rate to attend. The participants get to play golf with an athlete, and prizes and dinner accompany this all-day event.

SAMPLE FOUNDATION

The Hole-in-One Foundation was created to raise awareness of the ongoing fight against illiteracy in the inner cities. Each year, founder Kermit Pemberton puts on a golf tournament to help in this battle. He emphasizes education and feels strongly about children's commitment to education.

The Hole-in-One Foundation is designed to help children make their own Holes-in-One. Every day children face sand-traps when battling situations of delinquency, drugs, violence, gangs, crime, and unemployment.

This is no easy task. The program's inner-city children live in communities where high levels of conventional literacy often are neither expected nor rewarded. Just stroking a golf ball in a hole with one swing is not enough. Kermit Pemberton, with the help of the community, hopes to "sand-bag reading disorders."

Going from kindergarten to 12th grade is a long-stroke situation. These grade levels often determine whether kids make it and go on to success or are forced into discouraging situations.

The foundation, founded by Kermit Pemberton in 1987, has achieved prominence in the Los Angeles community and growing respect on a national level.

Tour luncheon series

Luncheon meetings are held during the Professional Golf Tour. Kermit Pemberton and a visiting dignitary/sports celebrity speak to the community's Hole-in-One supporters. Hole-in-One children then make presentations.

Golf Camp

This is an outdoor program that helps youth learn the game of golf. It was created to promote extracurricular activities in a controlled environment, thereby challenging children physically and mentally by promoting learning abilities.

Storytellers' Program

The winter program hires and trains teens 14 to 16 years of age to read stories to younger children at child-care agencies in the Los Angeles City Library District. The program enhances the literacy development of the children as well as the teenagers.

**The Pemberton Hole-In-One Foundation Golf Classic
and Sports Celebrity Weekend**

**Los Angeles City Golf Course
December 1-3
SAMPLE**

Sports Stars
Each team will be joined by a celebrity golfer.
BIG ED THOMAS
JOE MORRIS
DERRICK THOMAS
NIEL SMITH
BRODERICK THOMAS
CHRIS SANDERS

ENTRY FEE:
$5,000.00 per team
(A team will consist of 4 amateurs and 1 celebrity)
ENTRY FEE INCLUDES:
- **4 golfers and surprise packages**
- **4 tickets to Friday Night Pairing Party**
- **1 table of 8 to All Star Banquet**
- **8 celebrity-autographed golf balls**
- **10 celebrity-autographed hats**

FOR MORE INFORMATION, PLEASE CALL:
Sports Services of America™
(310) 821-4490
**A well-organized tournament can raise anywhere from $25,000
to $250,000.**

Kids in Sports of Los Angeles has received $604,000 from the Amateur Athletic Foundation, which provides year-round sports programs at 11 sites. More than 5,000 youths from inner cities participate in these programs. The grant was the largest of 25 handed to Southern California youth sports groups by the AAF of Los Angeles, which distributes funds from 1984 Olympic profits. In all, $1.18 million was disbursed.

The development of a foundation by an athlete instills values, trust, commitment, honesty, loyalty, integrity, and goodwill in the community. A foundation can increase the athlete's standing in the community on and off the court. Although we hear negative things about athletes, we should focus on the positive. There are many, many athletes who give time and money to organizations in their own hometowns or in the cities in which they play. This can enhance popularity, and more importantly, gain loyalty from the fans in the community.

Hole-in-One Foundation
Avoiding Sand-traps for Children
SAMPLE TOURNAMENT
The Kermit Pemberton
Hole-in-One Foundation
" Read ....Succeed"
"Learning to read can take a child a long way in life." **Big** *dreams for today's youth.*
Kermit Pemberton, Professional Golf Tour
Founder of the Hole-in-One Foundation

ONE-DAY SEMINAR

An athlete can promote his or her own one-day seminar. These seminars are designed to give participants instruction in a sport. The seminar is set up in stations, with each station designed for seminar participants to practice. For a one-day baseball seminar, an individual station is set up for hitting, another for fielding, etc.

There is a set schedule of instruction, broken down in individual groupings. For example, if a star baseball player was running an instructional seminar, he would set it up in sections. Section 1 would go over the elements of hitting with the group. Section 2 would talk about fielding. After the instructional discussion, the participants would practice the skills they have been taught at the appropriate station. These seminars are generally run for kids wanting to learn the fundamentals of a given sport.

Sponsorship: *Sponsorship fuels events.* Find title sponsors to help pay for some of the expenses in exchange for name recognition *(See Production of Special Event and Sponsorship sections).* This is usually a sure way of making your seminar financially successful. A baseball seminar may be sponsored by Louisville Slugger, in which case Louisville Slugger would supply the bats, balls, and batting gloves. A sponsor usually requires a complete proposal, including an advertising budget (See Sponsorship section).

Advertisement: The Sports section of the local newspaper is a good and reasonably priced location to advertise special events such as seminars. Other advertising may include national sport trade magazines, sport trade associations, and fliers at local gyms, courts, and courses. One-day seminars can be fairly successful financially; youth camps are much better, and they allow Mom and Dad a break.

Chapter 7

Broadcasting & Media

What is broadcasting?

The transmission of programs from a radio or television station. To speak, perform, or present on a radio or television program. Radio or television as a business profession. The business of transmitting entertainment by radio or television.

A historical overview of sportscasting:

RADIO

The prominent broadcaster in the early days of sports was Graham McNamee, who is known as the "father of broadcasting". McNamee was versatile enough to broadcast 10 sports.

McNamee's sportscasting career with NBC lasted 18 years. Some of his more famous broadcasts included The Dempsey-Tunney "long count" (1927), Babe Ruth's early World Series appearances, Earle Sande's third Kentucky Derby victory (1930), Glenn Cunningham's record-breaking mile at Princeton (1934), and countless football games, including the first coast-to-coast broadcast of the Rose Bowl. It was his 1923 broadcast, the Yankees vs. the Giants, over a three-state network (WEAF in New York, WCAP in Washington, and WMAF in South Dartmouth, Mass.) that put him in the forefront as the most prominent broadcaster of his time. His career spanned from 1923 to 1942.

Another sportscaster, who may not be as well known, is Major J. Andrew White. Records indicate that his first sportscast by radio was the Jack Dempsey vs. George Carpentier bout for the world championship on July 2, 1921, in Atlantic City, which drew 80,183 spectators and was the first million-dollar gate ($1,789,283) in boxing history. The fight was aired over WJY in New York. Dempsey knocked out Carpentier in the fourth round. However, some records indicate that to test the equipment, Major J. Andrew White announced a preliminary boxing match between Packy O'Grady and Frank Burns.

In September of 1923, Dempsey fought Firpo at the Polo grounds. You may wonder what a boxing match in the '20s sounded like. According to history, the dialogue sounded something like this:

"He's up. He's down. He's up. He's down." Who, you would wonder. Suddenly someone is flying out of the ring. White noted it was Dempsey, who ended up in the press section before returning to the ring. In the second round, however, it was easier to follow the fight. Needless to say, Dempsey knocked Firpo out.

A major contributor to the early history of sportscasting was KDKA in Pittsburgh. KDKA was owned and operated by Westinghouse. KDKA used "wireless telegraphy." A converted telephone was used as a microphone. KDKA was the first station to carry a baseball game, on Aug. 5, 1921 – the Pittsburgh Pirates vs. the Philadelphia Phillies. The game lasted 1 hour and 57 minutes. The Pirates were victorious, 8-5. The man who covered the game was Harold Arlin. He reflected on the game years later: "KDKA didn't even think baseball would last on radio. I did it sort of as a one-shot project, a kind of addendum to the events we'd already done." Arlin was the first baseball play-by-play man. He was also the first man to broadcast a tennis match (8/6/21) and to air a football game via the wireless – University of Pittsburgh vs. West Virginia.

The first football radio broadcast was on Nov. 25, 1920. Radio station WTAW broadcast a game between Texas and Texas A&M.

The first play-by-play of a World Series was the fall of 1921 by KDKA. Grantland Rice was the announcer. Tommy Cowan performed the first "re-creation" of a game over stations WJZ in Newark, N.J., and WBZ in Springfield, Mass. Cowan would listen to Grantland Rice announce the action over the telephone and recreate it without seeing the action. Recreations were quite common in the early days. With the help of ticker-tape reports of the action or phone relays, coupled with sound effects, recreations could sound quite real.

TELEVISION

In television today, companies work hard to become sports leaders. The 1996 baseball postseason was televised by four networks – NBC, FOX, ESPN, and ESPN2. Fox exclusively carried the World Series. The networks, in a collaborative effort, televised all post-season games.

On Nov. 1, 1996 Fox Sports America, in an effort to capture the Latin TV market, merged with Prime Deportiva and renamed it Fox Sports Americas. The new network will be Spanish-language and will reach 3.7 million homes in the United States and Latin America. Fox is aiming toward particular regions – parts of the United States, Mexico, Central America, the Caribbean. Brazil, and Argentina. Currently, Fox looks to expand. The station has affiliates in Asia, the United Kingdom, and Australia. ESPN

International, on the other hand, reaches 105 million homes in 160 different countries.

The first baseball game televised was on May 17, 1939, at Columbia's Baker Field. The first major league telecast was Aug. 26, 1939, at Strom Ebbets Field. The first football telecast, which turned out to be a college game, was on Sept. 30, 1939, a match-up between Fordham and Waynesburg (Pennsylvania). Fordham won 34-7.

The first pro football telecast was on Oct. 22, 1939 – the Brooklyn Dodgers vs. the Philadelphia Eagles. The Dodgers won 23-14. There were approximately 1,000 television sets in New York City. Fans today don't realize the impact technology has had on sports. In the first ever televised NFL game, there was one broadcaster and there were two cameras. Allan "Skip" Walz was the broadcaster: "It was a cloudy day, and when the sun crept behind the stadium, there wasn't enough light for the cameras... The picture would get darker and darker, and eventually it would go completely blank, and we'd revert to a radio broadcast... We used two iconoscope cameras. I'd sit with my chin on the rail in the mezzanine, and the camera was over my shoulder. I did my own spotting, and when the play moved up and down the field, on punts or kickoffs, I'd point to tell the cameraman what I was talking about. We used hand signals to communicate. The other camera was on the field, at the 50-yard line, but it couldn't move, so we didn't use it much."

The game reached approximately 500 TV sets. The game was broadcast over RCA's experimental television station, W2XBS. Compare that to NBC's coverage of the 1996 Olympics, for which an estimated 209 million viewers tuned in – a record.

One of the more interesting concepts in TV sportscasting was executed in 1996 by SportsChannel Ohio. The channel featured a commercial-free game. "This additional Indians telecast will allow SportsChannel to provide the local sports fan with a behind-the-scenes look at how our network brings the flavor of Indians baseball to the viewers at home," said David Kline, SportsChannel's senior vice president and general manager. The telecast ran features: How the baseballs are rubbed down with Mississippi mud before each game, the dynamics of a telecast, and how hot dogs are made. The concept was very well-received.

NBC's pioneering achievements in telecasting sports events accelerated after that. Firsts include the following:

Feb. 1940   Basketball (Pittsburgh-Fordham; NYU-Georgetown)

Feb. 1940   Hockey (New York Rangers vs. Montreal Canadians)

Dec. 1945 Football (Army-Navy on a network of four cities: New York, Philadelphia, Washington, Schenectady)

June 1946 Heavyweight Boxing Championship (Joe Louis vs. Billy Conn)

Sept. 1947 World Series (Brooklyn Dodgers vs. New York Yankees)

Oct. 1951 World Series coast-to-coast telecast (N.Y. Giants vs. N.Y. Yankees)

Jan. 1952 Rose Bowl coast-to-coast telecast (Illinois vs. Stanford)

Mar. 1954 Color transmission of boxing, Madison Square Garden, N.Y.

Aug. 1954 International live sports event (From Canada, "Miracle Mile" Roger Bannister-John Landy)

Sept. 1955 Color transmission, college football (Georgia Tech vs. Miami

Sept. 1955 Color transmission, World Series (N.Y. Yankees vs. Brooklyn Dodgers)

Nov. 1955 Color transmission, Army vs. Navy football

Aug. 1955 Color transmission, Davis Cup Tennis, Forest Hills.

COMPUTERS AND SPORTS

Access to the Internet allows fans to hear radio transmissions through their computers. In the future, games will be televised via computer. Currently some teams are already broadcasting games over the World Wide Web. The Seattle Mariners were the first team to simulcast on the web under an agreement between the team, radio station KIRO 710-AM, and Starwave. The Mariners' first cybercast was July 11, 1996. The Mariners were also the first pro sports team to establish a web site.

The 1996 Olympics teamed up NBC and Intel Corp. to create an inter-cast. Inter-cast was developed by Intel, utilizing computer technology for more complete Olympic coverage. The coverage included athlete backgrounds, event results, statistics, and rules and regulations. It also allowed users to score diving events, matching their scores with those of the judges, and to follow the leaders of marathon. The site included interesting facts, such as athlete hometowns, hobbies, and individual statistics. Users could participate in the hype of the Dream Team poll and read athlete biographies. The Internet will play a major role in sports as technology continues to develop. Technology assures access to more information, potentially changing the way we view sports.

Chat rooms on the Internet are similar to talk radio; fans have the opportunity to voice their opinions in a informal arena with other fans. Companies such as ESPN, SportsLine USA, and Sports Network are utilizing this technology as we move into the next millennium. It is hard to predict what the future will bring, but certainly the Internet will play an important role. Athletic organizations are setting up new web sites every day. The Internet will allow us to get as much information as possible, including player biographies, statistics, ticket prices, etc.

Currently, companies are beginning to work on measuring the effectiveness of Internet advertising. This will play a major role in who sponsors what site. More and more companies are beginning to get involved in developing Internet sites. During the Dodgers' 1996 postseason appearance, on their site you could see live video feeds. The technology was not to the point of allowing high-quality feeds, but the idea and concept will catch on quickly. During the 1996 National League playoffs, the San Diego Padres' site allowed visitors to hear the radio broadcast of the games in "real time."

PRINT MEDIA

The role of print media over the past decade has changed the world of sports. In the early days of sports, a "beat" reporter for the paper covered a team. There was a bond between the reporter and the athletes. This trust could not be broken, because if a newsman printed a negative story about what an athlete did the night before, there would be a price to pay. Loyalty and trust between the "beat" reporter and the athlete was understood.

Modern-day media disregard private issues, making everything public knowledge. Athletes need to realize that from the time they sign a contract or a letter of intent to attend a college, everything is fair game. The print media have one goal – to sell newspapers. Athletes in bold print sell newspapers. Media coverage is so extensive that if an athlete says the wrong thing, it will be analyzed, and things are often taken out of context. This should cause great concern for athletes. Media can cost athletes endorsements simply by printing negative words, which in turn affect the images of sports figures.

An athlete must realize the potential consequences of their actions and words. Fans feel that athletes owe them something. This is not the case. An athlete gets paid to perform. That is the bottom line. The media gets paid for headlines – it's as simple as that. These two entities realize the implications of their actions.

Influence Of Media

In modern sports, the media representatives are essentially the ones who vote for awards. In 1995, Mo Vaughn received the American League MVP award; controversial Cleveland Indian outfielder

Albert Belle was passed up for the award. Belle was the first man in the history of Major League Baseball to hit 50 or more doubles and 50 or more home runs in a single season. Belle is notorious for his explosive temper and negative reputation and image. He does not cooperate with the media. Did that cost him the MVP? Mo Vaughn, on the other hand, was more "media friendly." I personally felt Albert Belle was the MVP.

It helps when athletes and media respect each other's professions

These two entities are in business together. One cannot function without the other. Athletes and coaches, for the most part, are forced to hold press conferences or at least open the doors to reporters for interviews. Some athletes refuse to talk to the media, and this often leads to fines. The role of the media has become much more intense than ever before. Every move an athlete makes is news. Behind the scenes, leagues try to force athletes and coaches to give interviews, because these sports figures are parts of the product being sold by the league. Sometimes athlete are interviewed live after games. This does not give the athlete time to collect his thoughts or emotions. An athlete should always be prepared, whether he is talking to a media representative one-on-one, giving a press conference, or being interviewed on a live broadcast. He should be ready at all times for interviews, regardless of the situation.

The Occupational Side Of Sportscasting

The job of the broadcaster is to report the game and to report what he sees. In radio this can be especially challenging, since the listener does not have a visual aid. The broadcaster must somehow paint a picture of the action. The information must be clear and concise. In television broadcasting, the dynamics are different from radio because of the medium's visual nature; the audience has a visual image. The telecaster merely enhances the visual picture and adds insight about what the audience sees.

A post-game interview can be the most challenging job for a broadcaster. If a team wins the Super Bowl, going into their locker room can be an easy task. There is celebration, champagne, and hugs everywhere. Going into the defeated team's locker room can be a bit more difficult. What does one say? "What happened out there today, Coach?" His typical reply is "We lost."

Currently, broadcasters offer insight from locker rooms, including such features as injury reports or brief half-time interviews with a coach. Broadcasters are even permitted to be a part of an NBA huddle. The role of the media has changed mainly because whereas in the past there was only a play-by-play announcer and a color announcer, now additional on-field reporters are often included. A third and sometimes fourth sideline reporter adds depth and more complete coverage. I call this coverage "inside the game"; although it does not quite capture the emotion of the players, it has the ability to add tension to the drama.

Play-by-play announcer – Reports the action as it happens.

Ex: Marv Albert, John Miller, Dick Enberg

Color announcer – Adds insight and explanations relating to the action.

Ex: Bill Walton, Jim Kaat, Steve "Snapper" Jones, Bob Trumpy

The Color commentator is usually an ex-athlete or coach. The reason is simple – these people grew up around the game and played on a competitive level. Their knowledge and insight adds to the game. It gives the listener details and explanations, as well as possible team strategies. Monday Night Football utilizes three broadcasters in the booth. This tactic is becoming common, particularly in the postseason for all sports.

All broadcasters, and especially color commentators, must be knowledgeable about the sport. Sideline reporters have enhanced the broadcast of sporting events. An example of this was the coverage of the NBA Finals. Hannah Storm reported on the Chicago Bulls, while Ahmad Rashad reported on the Seattle Supersonics. This added new dimensions to the broadcast, including half-time reactions from coaches, game strategies, and insight from the huddle during time outs.

Keep in mind, broadcasting is a form of entertainment. Former NBA center Bill Walton constantly looks to make hype out of nothing, and some of his comments are so outrageous that they are laughable. John Madden, one of the more notable football color commentators, is also one of the real showmen of sportscasting.

Network sportscasters can be heavily compensated; however, there is no easy road to the top. Brent Musburger currently has a six-year contract with ABC for $11 million. He is TV sports' highest-paid announcer. The following are some statistics detailing annual salaries of sportscasters:

TV Sportscasters' Millionaires Club

<u>Annual salaries (in millions):</u>

Brent Musburger	ABC	$1.83
Al Michaels	ABC	$1.75
John Madden	CBS	$1.70
Pat Summerall	CBS	$1.50
Dick Enberg	NBC	$1.40
Bob Costas	NBC	$1.40
Frank Gifford	ABC	$1.20
Dan Dierdorf	ABC	$1.20
Tim McCarver	CBS	$1.20

How Does Someone Get Into Sports Broadcasting?

There are schools that specialize in broadcasting – the Connecticut School of Broadcasting is one such institution. The most common way to get started in the industry is through education, most often at the secondary level. Look for a school that offers an opportunity to get involved in radio and TV. This can become a most valuable asset. Most of the broadcasters, such as Bob Costas, have attended college. There are, however, other avenues to take. You can work as a volunteer for a local radio or TV station. If you are in college, each summer you should try to get an internship that will offer experience and build your resume. Networking is your most important tool. Go to trade shows and seminars to try to get exposure for your name and meet as many people as possible.

Qualities such as determination, perseverance, and persistence are great assets, and they are all necessary in the field. On the lower level, such as in high school, expect little or no pay. Build on each experience.

If you have attended or plan to attend a school or a program that gives you on-air experience, tape all your work. If you broadcast six football games, tape all of them. At the end, put together a "greatest moments in broadcasting" tape of your work. This should be no longer than six minutes. If you are putting together a TV audition tape, create it on ¾-inch tape. That will allow you not to lose generations in the duplication process. Realize the person reviewing does not have a lot of time. Keep it short – no more than eight minutes – and put your best stuff first. Illustrate versatility if you can. For a television audition tape, use a feature story as well as on-air spots. Always put your best performance in the beginning.

Your goal is to catch prospective employers' attention. Make sure that your work is professional and polished. Look for creative ways to market yourself. An example: Have baseball cards made up of yourself and put them on the inside of the tape so your face is showing, just as if you were a recording artist sending your tape out. *Be creative.* Remember, you are marketing yourself.

Chapter 8

The Development of a Special Event

The Football Extravaganza party was developed by IMAGES USA and Sports Services of America™. A revised interview with Scott W. Williams, director of development for IMAGES USA follows.

The Super Bowl is considered by many to be the biggest yearly sporting event. For Scott Williams, the preparation begins long before the event. For an event such as the "Legends Fantasy Party," many hours and much thought are required in planning for issues such as the perks, cost, and profit. An event of this magnitude cannot exist without all the bases being covered. Careful planning and evaluation for each sponsorship package is necessary to ensure that sponsors get their money's worth.

The first and most important aspect to take care of is media contacts. Radio stations and tickets have to be lined up in order to put it all together. We approach our current clients to find out their level of interest. They should have the option of reading the proposals. Then we target local companies in the Super Bowl city. Often this means cold-calling to find out the level of interest these companies may have.

The athletes that we invite play a large role in the Super Bowl experience. We look for athletes who understand the nature of a corporate environment, and don't mind signing autographs or having their pictures taken with clients. People love to be around athletes. We take advantage of this fact to make sure clients get what they pay for.

Contacting Media Outlets

It will be necessary to approach three or four radio stations. The radio stations bid on the event, and the event organizer looks for the most cost-effective package. The bids include descriptions of the running schedule – the time the spots will run; this is also known as an advertising schedule. This schedule stipulates the number of live mentions, pre-recorded promos and live promotions during the event. We want the station to treat the event as a Rolls Royce, not just another event. We look for creative approaches and feel that the more creative the approach, the more we get for our money. We ask ourselves: What are the perks? Will the station do a live remote broadcast from the party or additional air time dedicated to our event? It is important to promote the event as much as possible. That is why barter agreements with radio stations are so valuable.

The total package

When a radio station makes a bid, here is what we look for: What are they offering? Ideally, we like to work with radio stations in a barter agreement. We make them a partner and give them sponsorship. A barter agreement trades our sponsorship opportunity for radio spots. It's a win/win for both sides, and allows the event to include more promotional material. The promotional material includes live mentions, which promote our event and their station. Radio station sponsors will often organize on-air ticket giveaways for the event. The station itself has an investment when it is a sponsor, and this means it is likely to give the event more air time. This is beneficial to both parties.

Another very important detail is securing a venue for the event. If you don't secure a venue, then the event cannot take place. This is done well in advance, sometimes up to a year before the event takes place.

Demographics

We include demographics in our package. The importance of demographics is in determining the type of radio station or other media outlet to look for to sponsor an event. Demographics define the consumers of a given product. We try to match the theme of a radio station, such as classic rock, rhythm & blues, or adult contemporary, to the event. Each station has different demographics. Adult contemporary is going to be an older crowd, whereas classic rock may be more appealing to a younger crowd. *Demographics play a role in what companies will be willing to sponsor the event*, and what type of station would appeal to the event's target market.

For this particular event, we used words that are football related – "Field Goal Sponsor," "Touchdown Sponsor," and "Title Sponsor." These are three types of sponsors, and price is based on the total value of a media package. We include two things – the retail price of the event and the sales price. We show sponsors what they are getting and how much it would cost them at a retail price. We want to illustrate the value of the overall package.

We break the deliverables down by categories for each level of sponsorship – advertising and promotion, hospitality and merchandising. We factor in the cost of everything when we determine the dollar value of the package. We estimate the actual value of the package to illustrate the savings to the companies that sponsor the event.

Advertising and Promotion

These categories cover exclusive rights for each sponsorship and what the sponsor gets in the way of advertising and promotion. This is what we do for them. It's a selling point we utilize for each level of sponsorship.

Hospitality

The hospitality component allows the sponsor to give tickets to employees and clients, and possibly to use the tickets for promotions and sweepstakes. These are deliverables that come with the sponsorship package. This also covers accommodations and logistics such as transportation, lodging, and tie-ins. What we need to do is to take care of the client/sponsor. These features increase the value of a given package. This is used in addition to media.

Merchandising

We always include merchandising in our sponsor proposals. This allows a sponsor exclusivity and the opportunity to see what is included in the package. It could possibly allow a company to put together a raffle or offer a free product sample or sweepstakes.

We also include the number of *gross impressions* – this measures the impact of the media package. Gross impressions include radio spots, and are not limited to just visual impressions. Most people think of gross impression as a subliminal message. Gross impression is measured in radio by the approximate number of listeners at a given time. The time when the station has the most listeners may be between 7-9 a.m., or at commuting time, 5-6:30 p.m. So when we include in our proposal estimations of the media value and number of gross impressions, we are mainly looking at radio spots the stations have allocated for promoting the event. Also, these estimations will give us an idea of how many times per day the sponsor will be mentioned. This carries leverage in the package.

Sample Proposal to Establish Sponsorship for the "Legends Fantasy Party"

INTRODUCTION

From the Creators of the LEGENDS EXTRAVAGANZA held in Atlanta in '94, Miami in '95, and Phoenix in '96

IMAGES USA, in conjunction with Sports Services of America™, Presents...

"Legends Fantasy Party"

Hosted by football greats

Joe Morris and Jim Kiick

"The Legends Fantasy Party" will be a spectacular gala to celebrate one of the greatest sporting events of 1997 – Super Bowl XXXI. It will feature live entertainment, dancing, special drawings, a cocktail reception, and celebrity appearances by NFL players and Hall of Famers. Sit and talk with an NFL legend. Pose for a photograph or lift a toast to the "good ole days" of football at its best. Come join in this festive occasion!

The "Legends Fantasy Party" will generate excitement and a sense of camaraderie amongst the visiting sports fans and the New Orleans community. This Fantasy Party promises to be one of the most sought-after events for entertaining guests and clients during the week of the Super Bowl.

Your sponsorship of the "Legends Fantasy Party" will help solidify (COMPANY) as an industry leader and advocate of community involvement nationwide while entertaining and rewarding key clients and personnel. The "Legends Fantasy Party" is certain to be a terrific, spirit-driven affair, and an exciting prelude to Super Bowl XXXI.

The "Legends Fantasy Party" is a unique opportunity for (COMPANY) to showcase its products and services and impact thousands of potential consumers who are residents or visitors of the New Orleans area. (COMPANY) can create a lasting favorable impression upon a significant number of potential customers, whose annual buying power exceeds $10 billion, by using this event as part of a creative marketing strategy. Experience the thrill of one of the world's greatest sporting events. Join the excitement and festive atmosphere. Witness the "Legends Fantasy Party!"

Demographics

"The Legends Fantasy Party" is a unique opportunity for (COMPANY) to impact thousands of potential consumers with the following demographics:

55%	Male
45%	Female
Age Range	25-65
Average Age	35-50

Super Bowl XXXI is predicted by many analysts to be one the largest Super Bowls in recent history. More than 150,000 visitors will generate more than $150 million for the local economy, with an average stay of four days, spending an average of more than $200 a day. Visitors descending upon the New Orleans area will include corporate executives, politicians, celebrities, and avid football fans who will come just "to be a part of the excitement." It is estimated that over 2,500 accredited media will visit New Orleans, while more than 130 million domestic and 750 million worldwide viewers will watch the Super Bowl via television and satellite.

Event Overview

Date: Jan. 24, 1997

Time:	8 p.m.-12 a.m.
Location:	French Quarter - TBA
Capacity:	2,000
Reception:	Complimentary hors d'oeuvres
	Cash bar
	Special door prizes
Entertainment:	Live and
Admission:	$100 per person

FIELD GOAL SPONSOR

$10,000

As Field Goal Sponsor, (COMPANY) will enjoy a valuable partnership role in the "Legends Fantasy Party."

As Field Goal Sponsor, (COMPANY) will be able to showcase its products and services via an exciting football-theme event, and advertise at a classic sports event. The Field Goal Sponsor package offers an outstanding opportunity for (COMPANY) to be a part of a creative community relations campaign.

Advertising and Promotion

- Naming rights as official Field Goal Sponsor of the "Legends Fantasy Party"
- Event identification with visible banners at the event
- Product or service sampling and display opportunities
- Advertising, public relations, and promotional activities
- Limited sponsor mentions during the "Legends Fantasy Party" event
- Rights to advertise, promote, or publicize sponsorship using the exclusive "Legends Fantasy Party" logo
- First right-of -renewal as a Field Goal Sponsor for 1998

Hospitality

- 2 Sponsor tickets to Super Bowl XXXI
- 10 Sponsor tickets to the "Legends Fantasy Party"
- VIP Reserved Sponsor Seating at the "Legends Fantasy Party"
- 25 tickets to the NFL Experience
- Photo opportunities with NFL alumni, players, and celebrities

Merchandising

- Promotions to leverage sponsorship, including sweepstakes, non-profit tie-ins, giveaways, etc., may be developed
- Merchandise opportunities with select vendor apparel

Estimated Media Value of $25,000, with over five million gross impressions.

TOUCHDOWN SPONSOR

$25,000

As Touchdown Sponsor in a specific product or service category, (COMPANY) will enjoy an exclusive valuable partnership role in the "Legends Fantasy Party."

As Touchdown Sponsor, (COMPANY) will be able to showcase its products and services via an exciting football-themed event. The Touchdown Sponsor package offers an outstanding opportunity for (COMPANY) to get involved, particularly at a "grassroots" level.

Advertising and Promotions

- Naming rights as official Touchdown sponsor of the "Legends Fantasy Party"

- Sponsor name is featured on select advertising, brochures, collateral materials, invitations, posters, and program covers

- Prominent event identification with highly visible banners at the event

- Exclusivity in specific product or service category

- Product or service sampling and display opportunities

- Advertising, public relations, and promotional activities, including radio and print media

- (COMPANY) representative recognition on stage at the event

- Some sponsor announcements during the "Legends Fantasy Party" event

- Right to advertise, promote, or publicize sponsorship using the exclusive "Legends Fantasy Party" logo

- First right-of-renewal as Touchdown Sponsor for 1998

Hospitality

- 4 VIP Sponsor tickets to Super Bowl XXXI

- 25 VIP Sponsor tickets to the "Legends Fantasy Party"

- Complimentary drink tickets

- VIP Reserved Sponsor seating at the "Legends Fantasy Party"
- 60 tickets to the NFL Experience
- Autographed memorabilia signed by NFL players

Merchandising

- Promotions to leverage sponsorship, including sweepstakes, non-profit tie-ins, giveaways, etc., may be developed
- Merchandise opportunities with select vendor apparel
- IMAGES USA agrees to recommend (COMPANY) to any spectators or other event sponsors requesting said services.

Estimated Media Value of $40,000, with over 10 million gross impressions.

TITLE SPONSOR

$50,000

- The exclusive naming rights as the official Title Sponsor of the "Legends Fantasy Party"
- (COMPANY) featured on all advertising brochures, collateral materials, invitations, posters, program covers, and table tents
- Prominent event identification with highly-visible banners

- Exclusivity in specific product or service category
- Product or service sampling giveaways and display opportunities
- Advertising, public relations and promotional activities, including radio and print media
- (COMPANY) representative recognition on stage at the event
- (COMPANY) sponsor announcements throughout the evening at the "Super Legends Fantasy Party" event
- Right to advertise, promote, or publicize sponsorship using the exclusive "Legends Fantasy Party" logo
- Customized promotions to leverage sponsorship, including sweepstakes, non-profit tie-ins, giveaways, etc., will be developed at sponsor's request.
- First right-of-renewal as Title Sponsor for 1998

Hospitality

- 10 Sponsor tickets to Super Bowl XXXI
- 50 VIP Sponsor tickets to the "Legends Fantasy Party"
- Complimentary drink tickets
- VIP Reserved Sponsor Seating at the "Legends Fantasy Party"
- 100 tickets to the NFL Experience
- Autographed memorabilia signed by NFL players
- Photo opportunities with NFL players, alumni, and celebrities

Merchandising

- Promotions to leverage sponsorship, including sweepstakes, non-profit tie-in, giveaways, etc., may be developed

- Merchandise opportunities with select vendor apparel

- Exclusive right to feature logo on select merchandise

- IMAGES USA agrees to recommend (COMPANY) to any spectators or event sponsors requesting said services

Estimated Media value of $100,000, with over 20 million gross impressions.

Marketing And Media Plan

The marketing and media plan for the "Legends Fantasy Party" will include local and regional coverage via radio and print media to obtain as much exposure as possible for corporate sponsors. (Each sponsorship level reflects the number of audience impressions and the media package.)

Radio

Promotional opportunities will be developed by IMAGES USA with radio stations to promote the event. Targeted stations include:

KLJZ, 106.7 FM	WNOE, 101.1 FM
WEZB, 97.1 FM	WQUE, 93.3 FM

WLMG, 101.9 FM   WRNO, 99.5 FM
WYLD, 98.5 FM

Print

Local and regional advertisements will be placed in high-circulation papers and magazines several months prior to the event to create public awareness and generate corporate ticket sales. Targeted publications include:

The Times-Picayune   *Gambit*

The Clarion Herald   *New Orleans*

Data News Weekly   *Louisiana Weekly*

Title, Presenting and Touchdown Sponsors will receive print exposure based on sponsorship levels.

Advertising/Promotions/Merchandising

Customized programs will be developed to leverage (COMPANY) sponsorship including sweepstakes, on-air giveaways, apparel and football accessories such as footballs, T-shirts, caps, and other promotional items.

Invited Guests...

- Billy "White Shoes" Johnson
- Derrick Thomas
- Dwayne Joseph
- Chris Sanders
- Broderick "Sandman" Thomas
- "Big" Ed Thomas
- Neil Smith
- ...and many more

Many of the sports celebrities will be dressed in their original game jerseys or team apparel. At the party, many of the guests will be entertained by a 5- to 10-minute story of past football experiences by our celebrity guests. (COMPANY) will have a reserved table with its company name or logo on the table for its employees and invited guests and will have the opportunity to pick a special guest to sit at its table. There will also be photo opportunities throughout the weekend.

Chapter 9

The Women's Sports Market

The women's sports market is estimated to be worth $10 billion a year. It is one of the most lucrative markets. The number of U.S. women participating in sports is higher than ever. Women represent 55% of all frequent fitness participants and 53% of all health club members. They represent over half of all volleyball players, 45% of tennis players, and 43% of runners, hikers, and tent campers. They represent 41% of all softball players, 39% of downhill skiers, and 36% of those who train with free weights. Women purchase 53% of athletic shoes, 68% of stationary bikes, and 66% of stair-climbing machines. Besides purchasing sports items for themselves, women are the key sporting goods shoppers for children.

The Growth of Participation in Women's Sports

In 1971-72, about 30,000 women participated in college sports. By 1994-95, that number was 110,000. During that same period, female high school athletes jumped from about 300,000 to over two million—about one of every three girls. Great UCLA basketball coach John Wooden has said he admires the growth of women's basketball. He states, "I feel that the best pure basketball is now being played below the rim, with finesse and beauty, by the very best women's teams. In contrast, men's basketball has become too individualistic and focused on showmanship."

1994 Women participants (millions)

Volleyball	**8.9**
Basketball	**7.7**
Soccer	**4.3**
Baseball	**2.8**
Football	**2.4**

The underrepresented women's athletic market is growing fast. Long-range demographic trends in American marital and family life show that working women's participation in sports and fitness activities is likely to expand in the future. Basically, women are going to have more time to enjoy sports. There has been a drop in the number of married households, a decline in the number of households with children, and an increase in men sharing housework, giving married women more time for sports. Also, in 1970, one in every 27 girls played in varsity sports. Now, it's one in three.

Don't underestimate the number of women who watch sports. The growth of women spectators has been increasing. In a 1994 Sports Services of America™ poll of 1,000 women, ages ranging from 18 to 52, interviewed over a six-month period between August and January, 300 women said they followed the NFL. Some do not follow it as closely as men do, but they do watch. Also, 360 women watched major league baseball and 340 watched NBA basketball.

The 1995 *Sporting News* list of the "100 Most Powerful" sports figures lists Donna Lopiano of the Women's Sports Foundation at #41; Sara Levinson, president NFL Properties, at #72; and Liz Dolan, Nike vice president of marketing, at #97.

An example of a successful athlete is top female race car driver Lyn St. James. She has set 31 national and international speed records during her 15-year career. Her awards include "Rookie of the Year" in the Indianapolis 500. She has been a consumer adviser and spokesperson for the Ford Motor Company since 1981. She has also been featured in a full-page ad for Rolex watches and has endorsed Revlon, Jantzen, JC Penney, and Nike. She has authored *The Lyn St. James Car Owner's Manual*.

Lyn St. James' success in endorsements illustrates the fact that some companies are beginning realize that there is money to be made by marketing successful female athletes.

There Are Several Reasons Why The Women's Sports Market Is Ripe For Advertising Dollars:

- The market for men's sports has become saturated, and women's sports provide a unique sports audience.

- The women's sports events generally have fewer sponsors, which means less ad clutter.

- Women's sports attract more family-oriented audiences – young professionals with daughters, and older retired persons with high levels of disposable income.

- Women represent half the population, but 70% to 80% of the buying power.

- Women are more likely than men to be brand loyalists.

As the number of sponsor dollars per event increases, there will be a growth in the female market. Sponsors are now looking for less expensive events to sponsor that will give them solid returns. The female market may be the alternative market sponsors are looking for. Women's sports are on the rise, which means TV exposure and sports features promoting women will increase. Companies are beginning to recognize the market value offered by women's sports.

One of the growing high-profile sports women are now participating in is Women's Professional Basketball. The NBA has organized a Women's National Basketball Association (WNBA) in eight cities. The WNBA has television contracts beginning in 1997 with ESPN and Lifetime. Each network has agreed to broadcast one live weeknight game, in addition to playoff coverage continuing throughout the season. It will be Lifetime's first live sports broadcasts. NBC has also signed on. Another league competing with the WNBA is the American Basketball League (ABL), also in eight cities. The ABL has signed 10 players from the U.S. Olympic women's basketball team. The ABL has signed a deal with SportsChannel Regional Network. The coverage will include 14 regular-season games, the ABL All-Star Game, two playoff games, all potential clinching games, and the ABL Championship. The network can carry up to 20 regular-season games. SportsChannel will also make ABL games available to

Prime Sports. Tip-off was in October 1996. The WNBA starts in 1997. This will be great exposure for women's sports.

Although in the past women's professional basketball did not succeed, the tie-in with the NBA ensures a fighting chance. For young ladies across the country, the exposure of these leagues offers great promise. The television exposure alone could shape the next generation of women athletes. It will give young girls a chance to dream of one day playing professional basketball.

NBA Commissioner David Stern had this to say: "ESPN delivers the strongest male demographics on cable, Lifetime delivers the strongest female demographics on cable, and NBC delivers the highest overall sports rating on television. These agreements ensure that the WNBA will receive the most extensive coverage of any sports league in its first season in history."

Women's participation in the Olympic Games has increased in every Olympics since 1896, when there was just a handful of women. In 1996, 3,779 women participated – an increase of 40% from the Barcelona games of 1992. One of the most positive effects the Olympics offer women and girls is the creation of sports heroes and athlete role models. Females who don't receive equal television coverage get moments to shine in the Olympics. Girls see role models and relate to athletes such as Jackie Joyner Kersee, Gail Devers, and Teresa Edwards. Former collegiate standout

Rebecca Lobo, who participated on the 1996 U.S. women's basketball team that won the gold medal, received a great deal of press and exposure when UConn's basketball team went an incredible 31-0 in 1995-96. She was also one of the finalists for *Sports Illustrated*'s Athlete of the Year award for 1995.

It is not difficult to recognize the positive effects of women's participation in sports. According to the Women's Sports Foundation and Wilson Sporting Goods, girls active in sports are:

- 92% less likely to experiment with drugs.
- 80% less likely to have teen pregnancies.
- Less likely to be depressed.
- More likely to feel positively about their bodies.
- Three times as likely to stay in school.

Nike ran an ad campaign that utilized the positive findings about women's/girls' participation in sports. Gillette is one of the companies that realized the potential market share to be gained by advertising through women's sports. Already a strong advertiser in men's sports, Gillette has started to spend advertising and sponsorship dollars on women's sports. Gillette has also teamed up with Sprint in promoting phone cards, with 17 collectible cards spotlighting the women's basketball Final Four tournament. Spalding sporting goods has also entered the women's market, introducing a division geared toward women's sports. Nike ran a

TV ad promoting women's sports. Companies realize the potential business to be generated by targeting the female market.

Still, many marketers and advertisers fail to recognize this growing market share. Some of their mistakes include:

- Failing to recognize the diversity in the women's market. There are actually three types of women to sell to: recreational athletes, amateur athletes, and professional athletes. Each market segment is unique and should be handled that way.

- Ignoring the philosophical barrier that still exists between how athletic women behave and how they describe themselves. Most women, except for the elite and nationally ranked athletes, aren't comfortable calling themselves athletes. This needs to be taken into consideration when an ad campaign is developed for this particular market.

To succeed, marketers and advertisers should:

- Use sports to appeal to women through consumer education, grassroots targeting, support for causes important to women such as breast cancer research, and ads honoring women's achievements.

- Focus on an athletic lifestyle, not necessarily the individual. Show how a product will benefit a woman and be useful, rather than positioning it as an athlete's product that she should buy because she's an athlete.

- Make products for women very different in style, fit, function, and design from those made for men. Golf and tennis players are screaming for style, fit, comfort, and performance instead of a smaller-sized, pink version of a man's product.

- Spend time, money, and energy designing or redesigning products to fit women's proportions. See how differently a woman uses your product and sell to her accordingly.

Sports Services of America™ Phone Survey

It is important to know what sports women are participating in, but it is equally important to know what sports they watch. In our recent survey, in which 100 females and 100 males participated, 29% of women polled like to watch NFL football, compared to

49% of the men. Women were more likely than men to name such sports as tennis, golf, and figure skating as their favorite sports to watch.

Chapter 10

Marketing Sports Event Tickets

Ticket Services Distribution

There are four major ticket distribution companies. These companies distribute tickets via telephone and computer modem at thousands of outlets nationwide. The companies produce catalogs of monthly events nationwide. There is usually a $300-$400 setup fee. Distribution companies charge 3-4% of the face value price of each ticket sold. There may also be a charge fee of 25 cents for each ticket that is printed and not sold.

These companies produce catalogs nationwide, offering an owner or promoter the opportunity to advertise to a broad target audience.

Marketing Sporting Event Tickets To Retail Customers

I will never forget my 19th birthday. I was so optimistic. I opened a retail sports promotion company specializing in sporting events. I advertised in newspapers, over the radio, and in the Yellow Pages. My customers were working-class people. I delivered tickets and other sports promotional items. I worked long hours to accommodate my customers and get them the tickets they desired.

It was hard work for small profit. The one drawback was the fact that my customers had a limited amount of money to spend. At the most one customer would spend $600 per year with me. It cost me $300 in advertising to get that customer and $200 to purchase tickets for that customer. This left me with $100 of profit, and I had to answer about 15 phone calls for every two tickets I sold – an inauspicious ratio.

Marketing Tickets To Corporations

My earnings with the general public were slim. I began marketing to corporations. In 1987, America's spectator sports ticket purchases totaled $7 billion. The majority of that $7 billion was accounted for by corporations using tickets as *incentives* and *premiums*.

My corporate promotions combined tickets with travel. The package included transportation, souvenirs, accommodations, and celebrity hosts. At first I charged 10 times cost, then 20 times cost – and purchases were still being made. It wasn't that I was charging so much. The scale revolved around elite events and national promotions. Businesses knew the value and potential tie-ins of having customers and employees attend major sporting events and top sports entertainment.

The Advantages Of Marketing To Corporations

The bulk of commercial business is repeat, unlike retail, which is limited by fans' budgets for high ticket items, which include major sporting events such as the Super Bowl, Final Four, Wimbledon, etc.

- They want the best.

There is no way to cut corners on the elite events. The elite events demand a higher entertainment dollar for a higher value of association. The intangibles of associating with events such as the Final Four, Super Bowl, World Series, and Indy 500 are endless (*success, loyalty, commitment, and perseverance, just to name a few*).

- Corporations planned what events they wanted to attend on an average 3-9 months in advance, which made for easy planning.

I have up to one year to plan for a major sporting event. Corporations plan their entertainment budgets 6-9 months before an event. Retail clients call days and even hours before an event to order. The retail client is looking more for the tickets to tomorrow's events – instant gratification. The corporate client looks down the road to the big events, planning his gratification months and years in advance. Corporations take the game a lot more seriously than normal fans, since they have more to gain.

- The corporate customer was a repeat customer – I didn't have to look for new customers.

This is the biggest advantage. Repeat business is the best business. There is no additional advertising cost. Fliers, newspaper ads, Yellow Pages ads, and radio ads are big expenses. With one phone call, I can sell 100 promotions – the equivalent of fielding 1,500 retail calls.

Fans demand value

I followed a hot young baseball prospect everywhere he went. The stadium was sold out everywhere he went. Spring training tickets for the bleacher seats, which had a face value of $2, were now worth $10 and sometimes even $15. Boy, did this player pack 'em in. This guy could hit the baseball over 500 feet. He was big! He was strong! He was young! He was new! He was the best ever and the fans loved him! The situations were unreal, considering the fact that that team was thought to be one of the worst on the planet.

I started a relationship with the ticket manager. He explained to me that the team had a really hard time selling tickets the previous season, and he thought the owner was selective in spending his money on players. I submitted a proposal that explained how I could help promote game ticket sales through sport programs and by putting up the money for tickets in installments. They offered me a deal in which I could buy season tickets and trade all of them for one game, and if I could not sell the tickets for that game, I could trade them for another game. This was an offer I could not refuse!

I advertised tour packages in the Sacramento area, which is a family-oriented community without a baseball team. I also sold my packages to incentive houses, which used customized programs to reward and entertain customers and employees. I worked with travel agents to organize small group travel programs. My customers loved the individual attention and service, and the customers rewarded us with gifts and thank-you letters. I still have over 20 Pink Panthers I received from Owens Corning Fiberglass.

- By the end of the 1990 baseball season, I had over 200 season tickets and the right to purchase 1,800 championship tickets. I could have sold over of $400,000 in programs at the same time.

Business continued at the same pace for three seasons. Then things began to change. It was the coming of the information age and some owners realized that their tickets were being resold for double the prices. They would take the information they got from the computer – all the numbers, statistics, and projections of profits – and call it PR and marketing. Did the computer tell them about excitement, privilege, loyalty, spirit, noise, and the smell of a sold-out game? They thought the bigger the stadium and the higher the cost per ticket, the more money the team could squeeze out of the local, hardworking fan, who was just looking for an escape from everyday life. Many of the owners thought corporate ticket buyers could afford high ticket prices, so they assumed they didn't need the working class fans to make their millions.

Let me be the first one to tell you that the little man creates the soul and sets the trends of the game – yes, the guy with a rainbow Afro who sits in center field, drinking beer and eating peanuts. Ultimately the fan is the end user of the product being sold by sponsors and advertisers.

Now the stadium is like an empty fish restaurant, no one wants to go in and eat an old piece of fish. The team is drawing just under 10,000 per game – down from 40,000 when I was a season ticket holder – and ticket prices have more than doubled. Why not ask the fans if they approve of the owner's ticket prices before raising them? Same with the players they traded – why not ask the fans?

Owners and promoters began with what I call scaling the house – charging more for better seating location and less for less desirable locations. Most of the action is between the lines in sports, and therefore those seats bring a higher demand. This technique revolutionized the entertainment industry, and gross ticket sales revenue nearly doubled within five years. In the future, tickets may fluctuate in price based on which two teams are facing off. However, it will be geared more toward the individual players. For example, the Chicago Bulls' Michael Jordan vs. The Los Angeles Lakers' Shaquille O'Neal will demand a relatively high ticket price. The star players will be the focus of ticket price fluctuation.

Chapter 11

Operation Costs and Ownership

1996 Olympic Games

Projected Revenue (millions)		Projected Expenditures (millions)	
Broadcast Rights	$555.5	Construction	$516.6
Domestic Sponsors	513.4	Operations	405.4
Ticket Sales	261.2	Executive Administration	182.9
International Sponsors	114.4	Sports and International Organizations	147.6
Merchandising	28.7	Operating Contingency	60.0
Other	107.5	Other	161.9
Total	$1,580.7		$1,508.7

Why Companies Purchase Luxury Suites

Approximately 75-85% of luxury suites are purchased by major corporations. Corporations use the suites to entertain key decision-makers, clients, and corporate brass. Luxury boxes are used as *premiums* and incentives that motivate customers and employees. The suites come with perks, which may include an open bar, free meals, and access to a restaurant on the suite level.

Here is a partial list of NBA/NHL franchises, where they play, and information about the income brought in from luxury suites:

Atlanta Hawks: A new arena seating 21,000 is to be built for the Hawks when they leave the OMNI. It will have 1,000 luxury box suites and 2,000 club seats. Prices were not released at the time of the press run for this book. Financing will come from a surcharge on rental cars in College Park and the city of Atlanta.

Boston Celtics/Bruins: The Fleet Center opened in 1995. It consists of 104 executive suites, the ticket sales for which are based on a 10-year lease and priced at four levels. The low end begins at $158,000-$170,000 and can go as high as $210,000-$248,000. When the Fleet Center opened, 91% of the boxes were vacant. The Fleet Center also had 2,526 club seats and three private restaurants.

Chicago Bulls: Built in 1994, the United Center consists of 216 luxury suites on three different levels. Luxury suite prices range from $55,000 to $175,000. The United center also has 3,000 club seats, which consist of eight rows on the club

255

level. The prices of the club seats range from $40 per ticket to a $1,000 *premium.*

Cleveland Cavaliers: The Arena at Gateway was built in 1994 and was later renamed the Gund Arena. It consists of 92 luxury suites with cost ranges between $85,000-$150,000. It also has 3,000 club seats.

Denver Nuggets/Colorado Avalanche: The Pepsi Center is scheduled to open in the fall of 1998. It will consist of 84 luxury suites ranging from $75,000-$135,000 and will also offer 1,000 club seats.

Detroit Pistons: In December of 1995, the Palace of Auburn Hills opened. It consists of 180 luxury suites that range in price from $40,000 to $210,000 per year. "Royalty seats" are offered for $6,500.

Los Angeles Lakers/Kings: The Great Western Forum currently offers no luxury suites, but it has 2,500 club seats ranging from $8,150 to $10,300 a year.

Milwaukee Bucks: The Bradley Center consists of 68 luxury suites, which bring in revenues ranging from $50,000 to $70,000 annually.

New Jersey Nets: Continental Airlines Arena has 29 luxury suites, which go for $150,000 a year and consist of 14 seats. At a price of $200,000 a year, 20 seats are available.

New York Knicks: Madison Square Garden has 89 luxury suites, which rent for between $250,00 and $300,000 per year.

Orlando Magic: The Orlando Centroplex was built in 1989 and expanded in 1995. It holds 26 skyboxes, which were available for $85,000 during the 1996-97 season. Those boxes come with a five-year lease and an annual price increase.

Philadelphia 76ers/Flyers: CoreStates Center opened Aug. 31, 1996. Luxury suites range from $75,000 to $155,000 and seat 12 to 14 people. The Center also has 1,500 club box seats, which go for $9,500 to $12,500 annually. One-third of these seats are limited to Flyers and 76er games only.

Toronto Raptors: There is a plan to build a 22,500-seat arena. It will consist of 84 luxury suites with license fees in the vicinity of $80,000-$130,000, along with 40 courtside lounges at $160,000 per year.

Utah Jazz: The Delta Center was opened in 1991 and has 56 luxury suites available on three- to five-year leases, with prices ranging between $65,000 and $150,000 annually.

Currently teams are looking to have new stadiums built, which would most likely increase revenue from luxury boxes. Luxury boxes alone bring in millions of dollars to individual teams. The Atlanta Braves worked out a deal to expand their luxury suites from 37 to 59, thereby increasing their revenue from $3.3 million to $10 million.

Team	Year Purchased	Price Purchased (in millions)	*Present Value (in millions)
Major League Baseball			
New York Yankees	1973	$10	$209
Baltimore Orioles	1979	$12	$173
San Diego Padres	1990	$75	$100
National Football League			
Pittsburgh Steelers	1933		$125
Dallas Cowboys	1989	$65	$272
Tampa Bay Buccaneers	1974	$16	$145
National Basketball Association			
Houston Rockets	1982	$10	$116
Phoenix Suns	1987	$44	$160
Orlando Magic	1988	$32	$100
Shaquille O'Neal	1996		$120

*Value fluctuates

Please note: In the summer of '96, free agency in the NBA caused salaries to escalate at an incredible pace. Shaquille O'Neal signed with the Los Angeles Lakers for an unprecedented $120 million dollars. This one contract had an impact on the entire industry. The Dallas Cowboys are the number-one franchise in sports, with an estimated value of $272 million dollars. Shaquille O'Neal's contract ranks #58. The #60 franchise is the Houston Rockets, with an estimated value of $116 million. Shaquille O'Neal's rank of #58 is higher than nearly half of all professional organizations, although his contract is measured over time. That is a remarkable impact.

Many professional sports franchises continue to earn profits despite labor problems and payroll pressures. In 1993, the Baltimore Orioles led all baseball clubs with an income of $26.9 million on revenues of over $80 million. The four components of a lucrative sports franchise are a huge market, a modern facility, shrewd proprietors, and strong management.

New venues

Many fans go to events that are planned in a new and exciting venue. Some venues are in high-traffic areas, and the high-profile events become self-promoting. This creates a lot of excitement for local fans, no matter what the neighborhood. The fans feel a sense of commitment, and they therefore reward the team with loyalty.

Mistakes Owners Make Regarding Venues

Over the last decade the United States and Canada have spent in excess of $2 billion for the construction of stadiums used by major professional sports teams. Factoring in the additional cost of stadium facilities currently under construction or in the planning stages, this amount could triple before the end of this decade. The attendance in newer stadiums has improved. The Cleveland Indians, Baltimore Orioles, Texas Rangers, and Colorado Rockies have also worked hard to improve personnel. Three of these four teams made the playoffs in 1996. However, there is no safe lead for the Rockies at Coors Field, where everyone seems to hit home runs. A new stadium doesn't make a team better, but it does increase attendance.

Many teams and franchises make the mistake of asking for a new venue when their team is defunct. At that point it is already too late for the stadium to receive approval and to provide an optimal benefit to the team. While the new stadium is being built, attendance drops off a minimum of 30% per season. Fans anticipate the new venue and don't want to go into the old, especially while the team is trying to save money and consequently offering second-rate entertainment.

Understanding The Word "Sell-Out"

Many owners do not understand the word "sell-out." They think it means to make less profit than they could have – "I could have sold more, so I am not charging enough." They don't understand that no one wants to go to a stadium that is empty. They don't understand the excitement, the togetherness, the smell and the noise level of a sold-out game. Ultimately, it's the consumer who will purchase products to be advertised by the team's sponsor. If the product doesn't sell due to low attendance and low exposure, advertisers won't advertise. Advertisers will find other alternatives.

Do The Owners Of A Team Spread PR For The Sport?

The owner can try to spread goodwill, but it is really hard for the average person to perceive an owner as hardworking and honest. The fans – the heart and soul of sports – usually do not relate very well to big business. The owner can more easily spread goodwill to the community business leaders, but it is just not the same; it's really not PR. Community business leaders do not represent the general public.

Some owners try to use tricks to project a positive image of themselves and their teams. For instance, an owner may publicize an athlete's salary offer, mentioning only broad terms of the offer and not telling the details, such as the fact that most of the money may be deferred. In this case, the owner hopes the public will then view the athlete as the bad guy for not accepting such a wonderful offer. Upon the athlete's refusal of the offer, the owner then goes to the public and can say, "Look, I am offering all·this money, but the athlete wants more. Our poor city!" Nowadays, this doesn't work as well, since everything eventually seems to be made public.

Another PR problem that hurts sports is when owners make headlines with negative aspects of their lives. Owners reflect upon the game just as athletes do. The media constantly looks for negative stories to write about those associated with sports.

What the owners should do to spread PR is work with the athletes. There is no "I" in "team." There needs to be unity. The fans relate better to the athletes; they respect and admire them. They want to be like Mike. By working with the athletes, owners can spread PR to people from all walks of life.

One way an owner can attempt to spread goodwill to the community is by playing a leadership role and being visible. This could include charity events and team-sponsored events for non-profit groups. Influencing community business leaders does not constitute affecting the general public. A good example of a well-loved and respected owner is the late Art Rooney Sr. of the Pittsburgh Steelers.

During the NBA spending frenzy in the summer of 1996, the Miami Heat signed Juwan Howard. Abe Polian, the owner of the Bullets (the team Howard played with prior to his departure), promised to match the amount of money fans donated to the Juwan Howard Foundation. Polian eventually kept his word after the disappointing departure of Howard. This was a generous act on the part of Polian, and it also promoted goodwill. The irony of the situation was that Howard's contract was voided by the NBA, and he was then resigned by the Bullets.

It is also wise to be very competitive. It's a very competitive business environment, and the very same people who praise you now may not give you a cup of hot soup next winter if your career collapses. I am not proud to say it. Winning changes everything – the bad image and the name-calling. The act of "winning" represents the spread of goodwill in today's society.

Chapter 12

An Inside Look at Bijan and Michael Jordan

Winning and Success

Birth date: February 17, 1963
Career highlights:

Became only the second player in NBA history to earn MVP honors in the NBA regular season, All-Star Game, and Finals in one year (1996).

Captured his record eighth NBA scoring title, 1995-96; earned seven consecutive scoring crowns, 1987-93; Career scoring average of 32.0 ranks as the NBA's best of all time.

Became only the fourth player in NBA history to record 2,000 career steals (vs. Miami, 4/4/96)

Reached the 24,000-point milestone for his career at New Jersey (3/16/96); he is one of only 10 NBA players to reach this mark.

Named NBA All-Star Game MVP in 1996 and 1988; voted to 10 NBA All-Star Games, 1985-93 and 1996

Averaged 26.9 points per game in 17 regular-season games following his return to the hardwood, and averaged 32.3 ppg in four postseason contests, 1995

Resigned with the Chicago Bulls on March 18, 1995

Joined Chicago White Sox AA affiliate Birmingham Barons, 1994

Announced his retirement from the NBA on October 6, 1993

Named league MVP in 1988, 1991, 1992, and 1996

Selected to the All-NBA first team eight times, 1987-93, 1996

Named to the NBA All-Defensive Team seven times, 1988-93, 1996; voted NBA Defensive Player of the Year, 1988

Earned NBA Finals MVP honors in each of the Bulls' championship seasons, 1991, 1992, 1993, and 1996

Scored NBA playoff record 63 points vs. Boston 4/20/86, and scored a career-high 69 points vs. Cleveland, 3/28/90

Became only the second player ever in the National Basketball Association to score over 3,000 points in a season

Voted NBA Rookie of the Year after leading the NBA in scoring, 1985

Selected by Chicago as the third pick overall in the NBA draft, 1984

Co-captain of the United States team that won the gold medal at the Los Angeles Olympic Games, 1984; member of gold medal-winning Dream Team, 1992

Earned All-American honors and was named College Player of the Year, 1983, 1984
Member of university of North Carolina's NCAA Championship team while being named Atlantic Coast Conference Rookie of the Year, 1982

By marketing an exclusive line of Michael Jordan-endorsed cologne, Bijan expects to sell well over $150 million worth of fragrance. Some industry insiders say $500 million could be closer to the actual sales total for the venture.

I had the honor of a sports marketing chat with Sondra Love, a senior marketing representative of Michael Jordan cologne who was the first person in 1991 to approach Jordan with the idea of going into business with Bijan. Here I am, a seasoned veteran of the money side of sports with almost 14 years in the business, talking with lady who put the estimated $150 million deal together. So I started Sondra out with what we call in baseball talk an "Uncle Charlie" – slang for "curveball."

Q: How would the cologne sell without Michael Jordan's name on the bottle?

A: This is an award-winning fragrance, and a lot of investment was made before launching. We focused on a group from the age of 16 to 34. We did mall intercepts and much, much more. You would not believe how much went into this award-winning fragrance – so much.

Q: Why Michael Jordan on a bottle of Bijan cologne?

A: Any time quality, credibility, and longevity are involved, you are going to end up with a winning formula.

Q: How much of Michael Jordan Cologne do you anticipate selling?

A: $150 million in 15 months from 1996 to 1997. We now have a strong indication based on domestic distribution that we should definitely reach that. There is talk about taking the fragrance international, but for now it is only talk. We have had a lot of requests, especially from Japan.

Q: What does Michael Jordan have to do with fragrance?

A: Everything. Michael loves to dress in style. He loves to get his manicures done every 10 days. He's clean. You see, Kermit, not everyone can glide though the air like an eagle like Mike can on the basketball court. Not too many people can duplicate that. But off the court, Michael and Bijan wanted to create a light-like-an-eagle, fresh-and-clean fragrance, just like Mike. I'm wearing it now. It's just so great! Now anyone can glide through the clean, fresh air. By the way, Kermit, Bijan plans to build Michael Jordan a $3 million wardrobe.

I am almost 51 years old, Kermit. I have been working since I was 13 years old. We have the X and the Y generation upon us, with no one to relate to. Along comes Michael Jordan. They need someone they can relate to.

This is the first product to bear Michael's name on it exclusively.

Michael said, "Sondra, I want my fragrance to have that newness feeling. I put on a new pair of shoes every game because it makes me jump higher and feel better."

I hope your book is a big success. It should be. Michael Jordan is one of the brightest business individuals I have ever been associated with or worked with. Let me just give you one example: out of eight attorneys reading a particular document, Mike was the only person to find a typo in the document. And to this day he still jokes with me about that typo.

In looking back to 1991, I remember one guy saying, "I can get you 20 top guys to choose from who would love to do this thing.

Let's just do it and sell the damn fragrance." You have to have the right person and if you have the opportunity to work with Michael, do it. He is just brilliant. It's very important that your people have a good business mind, Kermit. I hope your book will help and do a lot of people good.

In a survey conducted by Sports Services of America, 200 sports fans were asked who their favorite athlete was and why.

Who: 1. Michael Jordan

Why: 1. Winning and Success

Fans said they were most familiar with Michael Jordan. They could associate, relate, and establish a bond with Mike. Television and winning are largely responsible for Mike's visibility, and both winning and television go hand in hand.

I asked Dianna Brotarlo, fragrance consultant for the past seven years, "What does the smell of Michael Jordan Cologne mean to you?"

She replied, "Sweet and fruity smelling colognes are a trend of cologne that is becoming more and more popular. The sweet and fruity scent is more popular with:

1. Youths: age 16-26

2. The health conscious: People who watch what they eat and are concerned with what they consume.

3. Fitness people: People who exercise on a daily basis and are concerned with their appearance.

Fragrance consultants do not like to use the words "sweet" and "fruity." They prefer words such as "fresh" and "clean" because they do not want to limit their consumer audience."

Now let's take a look at the perfect marketing match and see why Bijan, Michael Jordan, and industry insiders expect to sell $500,000,000 worth of cologne.

Rare air

Striving for new atmospheric scents. Going beyond ozone, a popular ingredient for the '90s. It captures the actual environment at a Costa Rican Beach – tropical, dewy, and moist. Essences of cedarleaf, grapefruit, and lemon.

Cool

Interpreting Michael's favorite outdoor atmosphere at the Blue Ridge of the Appalachian Mountains in North Carolina. All-American freshness, crisp and clean. Essences of cypress, rosewood, geranium, and cognac.

Pebble Beach

Giving the olfactory experience associated with one of Michael's favorite pastimes, golfing at Pebble Beach. Early morning, brisk, freshly cut grass. Essences of clary sage, lavender, fir needles, and juniper berry.

Home Run

Capturing the scent from his baseball glove as he catches the ball. A new twist in leathery texture. Essences of green tea, clove leaf, suede, and incense notes.

Sensual

He's magnetic… He's sensual… He's unforgettable. Providing a sensual base that lasts and lasts. Essences of sandalwood, patchouli and musk.

All five accords coalesce as a single fragrance, and thus a masterful evolution occurs as the fragrance develops on the wearer.

The Hype of Michael Jordan and Bijan

MICHAEL JORDAN AND BIJAN FRAGRANCES ANNOUNCE GROUNDBREAKING PARTNERSHIP

Michael Jordan fragrance represents first product ever to bear athlete's name; agreement marks Bijan Group of Companies' first licensing endeavor

On the heels of his fourth NBA Championship with the Chicago Bulls, basketball superstar Michael Jordan has joined internationally renowned fashion and fragrance mogul Bijan in announcing a licensing agreement to create a men's fragrance line through XEL, Inc., a subsidiary of Bijan Fragrances, Inc. Michael Jordan Cologne, the first product to bear the athlete's name, also marks the first licensing endeavor by the Bijan Group of Companies. The fragrance line was launched in the U.S. in November of 1996, with a series of ancillary body products to follow in early spring of 1997.

Jordan, the first major male athlete in the U.S. to develop – and not simply endorse – his own fragrance, expressed his enthusiasm for the product and the partnership. "The scent isn't serious or contrived. It's relaxed and really makes you feel good. For me, that's a winning formula." He added, "This is a unique and truly fun project, one in which I have had a great deal of input at all levels. I have really enjoyed working with the Bijan Fragrances team because they genuinely understand the challenges of this project."

"For me, Michael Jordan represents the best of the best … in every respect. I admire and respect him for his great talents and for his integrity, enthusiasm, and spirit," stated Bijan. "As with my contemporary and more casual Bijan USA boutiques, I expect this new partnership to set the standard for many future projects appealing to a wide range of consumers. We in the fragrance business cannot ignore the enormous potential the younger generations offer as new customers."

Capturing the many facets of Jordan's personality and lifestyle, Michael Jordan Cologne blends five individual fragrance "accords": Rare Air, Cool, Home Run, Pebble Beach, and Sensual. Characterized as "light as air," the overall signature has a brightness and clarity that is both young and sexy, conveying the complexity of Michael Jordan and offering the wearer an elevated sense of confidence for every moment of his life.

According to Sondra Love, senior vice president of marketing and product development at Bijan Fragrances, "These five 'accords' blend as singular fragrance which shifts in response to the many moods experienced by the wearer throughout the day. To my knowledge, there has never been anything like Michael Jordan Cologne ever created." Assuring the integrity of the product, Jordan worked closely in the development of the cologne with the assistance of Givaudan-Roure Corporation, responsible for the multi-award-winning Bijan Perfume for Women.

Michael Jordan Cologne will be packaged as a natural spray, as well as an alcohol-free shower gel, deodorant, and body soap. The bottle and package design will reflect the elegance of Bijan and the diversity of Michael Jordan. Michael Jordan Cologne will be sold in prestige department stores and major athletic wear and sporting goods retail chains nationwide.

Michael Jordan, the charismatic Olympic gold medalist and Chicago Bulls guard, has been voted Most Valuable Player of the National Basketball Association four times (1988, 1991, 1992, 1996) and is one of the most recognized celebrities in the world, according to a recent Gallup survey. Jordan's product endorsement deals include those with Nike (Air Jordan shoes and apparel), Sara Lee Corporation, Quaker Oats (Gatorade), Rayovac (Renewal Batteries), Wilson Sporting Goods, LDDS-WorldCom (long-distance telephone service), Oakley (sunglasses), and Upper Deck (sports memorabilia and collectibles). He has made his motion picture debut in November '96 in the Warner Bros. live action/animated film "Space Jam," produced by Ivan Reitman. With a series of successful fragrances, including the award-winning classics Bijan Perfume for Women and Bijan Fragrance for Men, and two scents launched in May of 1996, Bijan Light for Women and Bijan Light for Men, the House of Bijan also includes Bijan USA, which marked the designer's first foray into the retail arena in 1993 with denim casual wear and accessories for men and women. Overseeing the very exclusive, "by appointment only" Bijan Designer for Men showrooms on New York's Fifth Avenue and Rodeo Drive in Beverly Hills, Bijan currently celebrates his 25th anniversary as the designer of choice to the world's rich and powerful, including five kings and 16 presidents. Most recently, he launched a $10 million international image campaign featuring actress Bo Derek in more than 82 countries.

MICHAEL JORDAN COLOGNE A SLAM-DUNK WINNER IN
SPORTING GOODS STORES

The House of Bijan, renowned for its "firsts" in the clothing and
fragrance industries, scored once again with its slam-dunk
distribution strategy for the new Michael Jordan Cologne, the first
fragrance ever to be developed – not simply endorsed – by a major
U.S. athlete.

In November, in addition to a traditional launch in major
department stores and national retail chains, Bijan Fragrances
introduced Michael Jordan Cologne in specialty sporting goods
and athletic wear retailers around the country. With over 46,000
such stores in the U.S. alone, Bijan Fragrances planned a
distribution strategy, setting a standard from which many are sure
to follow. Sportsmart, Footlocker, and Champs are among many
well-known national sporting goods chains to carry the new scent.
Michael Jordan Cologne is also featured in high-end retail chains
nationwide, such as Macy's, Dayton-Hudson, Marshall Field's, and
Dillard's.

"Consumers who purchase sporting goods products already
appreciate Michael Jordan, equating his name and image with
excellence. We decided to go to where our market already existed
and take advantage of the natural synergy between Jordan,
Renaissance man, and an adoring public who can't seem to get
enough of him," said Sondra Love, senior vice president of Bijan
Fragrance, which pursued Jordan over six years for this venture.
"Buying something as personal as cologne – and one created to his
exact specifications – is like connecting with Michael himself.
Placing this new product in environments which currently carry
other Michael Jordan merchandise will tap into a captive market."

Love sought an organization with national sales influence and
selected St. Paul, Minn., based Sports Distribution Professionals,

Inc. to carry out Bijan Fragrances' North American marketing and sales strategy for such a unique product. Founded 18 years ago by its president, Craig Darsie, along with partners Mike Donnelly and Michael Silvestro, the company has expertise pioneering new products, brands and concepts, and enjoys an outstanding reputation among specialty sporting goods retailers for its ability to assist dealers in the successful "sell through" of new products. Sports Distribution's principals have introduced the Avia line of athletic shoes (subsequently purchased by Reebok), Ultrawheels, the second largest in-line skate company in the U.S., and Sorbothane athletic insoles.

"Specialty sporting goods retailers have never carried a premium cologne. So for them, it's a big departure," according to Darsie. "What better way to introduce a new product than with the Michael Jordan name? Fortunately, we have established long-term relationships with our retailers and they recognize the enormous potential for Michael Jordan Cologne.

Sportmart, one of the country's largest sporting goods retailers for over 25 years, quickly signed on to be an anchor team member for the product introduction and roll-out. "Sportmart has a motto: 'Expect the unexpected.' We have never carried a cologne in our stores, and yet, this makes perfect sense," says Matt Powell, vice president of merchandising. "We carry merchandise which is both aspirational and inspirational. Our customers aspire to be like Michael Jordan, the greatest athlete in the world, and they purchase goods which inspire them to perform at their own peak levels."

Powell continues, "Michael Jordan takes care of himself. It shows in everything he does. He takes care of his body and his image. By owning Michael Jordan Cologne, our customers can share in that winning attitude and style. We know Michael Jordan Cologne will appeal to our customers, and with Bijan behind it, it will be high quality all the way."

"Michael Jordan commands our attention because he lives life to the fullest, excelling in everything he does and expressing our great style while doing it. Who better to emulate than this modern-day legend?" said Sondra Love. "We worked long and hard to consummate our relationship with Michael, and we feel confident that together, with Michael's valuable influence and creativity, we will premiere a fragrance which captures the elegance, playfulness, and zest which is Michael Jordan."

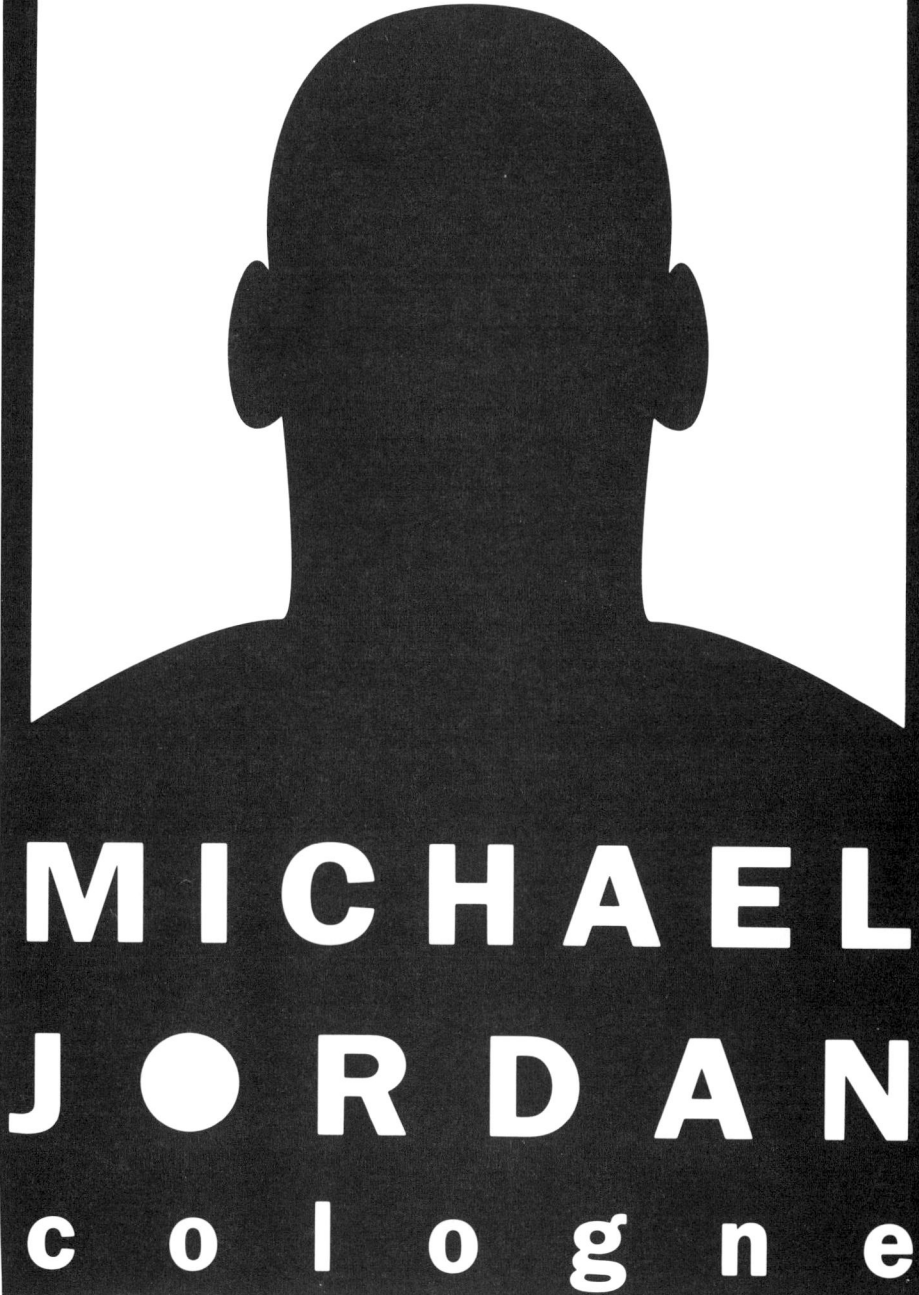

MICHAEL

J●RDAN

c o l o g n e

SYMBOLIZES NEW FRAGRANCE IDENTITY

Recent U.S. market surveys have proven that more people can positively identify an image of Michael Jordan than photographs of Princess Diana, Cindy Crawford, John Wayne, Whitney Houston, or even Bill Clinton. So it makes perfect sense that the House of Bijan selected a silhouette representation of Michael Jordan's head as the logo for his new fragrance, Michael Jordan Cologne, which made its U.S. launch in November, 1996.

"It's absolutely amazing! We went to malls all over the country and showed people pictures of all kinds of celebrities," says Court Crandall, creative partner of Ground Zero, the advertising agency responsible for designing the logo, print ads, and commercials for the Michael Jordan Cologne campaign. "People identified one or two images incorrectly, depending on their ages or backgrounds. But without fail, every single person recognized Michael Jordan, even in a picture with his back turned toward the camera."

When told of his overwhelming popularity, Jordan responded with typical modesty. "I can't believe more people recognize me than important world leaders. It's almost embarrassing."

Brian Tortora, Ground Zero's art director, suggested a simple silhouette for the Michael Jordan logo, based on the agency's belief that Michael is the icon and that a strong visual representation of him superseded the need for anything else. Moreover, agency creatives felt that a clean graphic likeness reflected the elegance for which Michael Jordan is known and would bridge all languages and cultures.

Zy Hafeez, director of worldwide advertising for Bijan, believes the power and simplicity of the Michael Jordan logo impacts the public as dramatically as the man himself. The logo also serves as the underlying vehicle for the creation of the Michael Jordan brand.

"The Michael Jordan Cologne 'teaser' campaign began with a 20' x 48' billboard which appeared on the San Diego Freeway, one of the nation's busiest. Additionally, 30-second introductory commercial spots appeared in movie theaters across the country on Oct. 7, as well as on national cable TV. National spot television commenced on Oct. 14. While the thrust of the campaign was television and radio throughout the remainder of '96, there will also be a print program as well," according to Hafeez.

Following the "teaser" campaign on Nov. 1, the formal fragrance campaign featuring Michael Jordan will premiere nationwide on television and radio. "It promises to be very exciting," says Hafeez. "It highlights a side of Michael the public has never seen before." The commercials were lensed by famed "got milk?" commercial director Kinka Usher. With the creativity handled by Ground Zero of Santa Monica, Bijan's $20 million advertising and promotional campaign for the introduction of Michael Jordan Cologne is expected to be one of the year's most successful fragrance launches.

MICHAEL JORDAN Q & A

Q. Why Bijan?

A. Quality, taste, perfection. I just think it's a perfect match. I have a certain way of doing things, and Bijan and I really understand each other.

Q. What is the concept behind your fragrance?

A. This is the first product with my name on it, so I wanted the fragrance to be exactly the way I like it… It's all about fun and feeling good!

Q. Who do you see wearing your fragrance?

A. Anyone who loves to live life the way I do! Have fun and feel good… all the time!

Q. Will Bugs Bunny wear your new fragrance, too? (Bugs stars in "Space Jam" with Michael Jordan.)

A. My cologne will smell better than any carrot ever did!

Q. Do you believe Michael Jordan would appeal to women, too?

A. I'm sure my wife will love it!

Q. How much will Michael Jordan, the fragrance, cost?

A. We're trying to keep it approachably priced. But it will definitely be less than a basketball!

Q. What does the fragrance smell like?

A. It's all about enjoying oneself. Michael Jordan Cologne will be as light as air… fresh, invigorating, and very sexy!

Q. Why would anyone want to wear your fragrance as opposed to a designer scent?

A. Why not? I do!

Q. With current market trends as they are, how will your fragrance stand out?

A. I believe you always need to be part of the winning team. You can't go wrong. Besides, success is based on quality, integrity, and longevity.

Q. We've seen so many 'celebrity' scents come and go. What do you believe will make Michael Jordan successful?

A. For one thing, no other fragrance has been this much fun! It's not serious or contrived. It's relaxed and really makes you feel good. For me, that's the winning formula!

Q. This is undeniably an interesting and unlikely partnership – sports and fashion. Off the court, will you be wearing any of Bijan's designs?

A. I love the way Bijan does things, and I'm thrilled we're working together. Maybe now I'll be on some best-dressed lists, too!

Q. Is Bijan going to design the next Bulls uniform?

A. Why not? But I doubt the Bulls could afford him!

Q. What do you think will make this a successful fragrance launch?

A. Quality! When people experience how good this cologne can make then feel, then we're a winner!

Q. What about other Michael Jordan products?

A. Well, we've gotta keep some secrets until the next time we meet!

Q. Has working with Bijan altered your perception of fashion in any way?

A. He's got an extraordinary eye for detail. And, while my wardrobe won't be complete for a few months, his designs have definitely given my personal style a big boost.

Q. Bijan, the man, keeps a low profile. There isn't much known about him, except for his signature ads. What is he like?

A. I guess he likes to be like many of his clients - private. He's really a great guy…charming, witty, and very intelligent.

Free publicity gives and adds more mentions of product. Surveys have shown that consumers are more likely to believe in a message if it is in a form of non-paid advertisement rather than a paid advertisement.

MONDAY, OCTOBER 14, 1996

USA TODAY

Money Money Money Money Money

Eau de Michael Jordan

Michael Jordan is trying to get in your face. And into your wallet. Again.

The world's most famous hoopster and product hypester has a new flick and a new fragrance on tap.

Call it Act n' Sniff.

Massive holiday marketing campaigns soon will try to coax you to dig deeply into your pocket and buy into Jordan's big-screen and small-bottle ventures. Michael Jordan, the unisex fragrance, hits the market Oct. 27, and will cost $23 a bottle. His upcoming movie, *Space Jam*, opening nationally Nov. 15, will have a galaxy of merchandise sold around it. Oh, did we forget to mention the NBA season begins in less than three weeks?

Welcome to the remarkable marketing of Michael. Increasingly away from sports. Forget Air Jordan. And Gatorade. And Ball Park Franks. Michael Jordan is being re-cast as Hollywood's best-smelling leading man. Corporate titans from Warner Bros. studios to Bijan fragrances are wagering millions that consumers will not only want to see Mike on the big screen but smell like him, too. It's a good bet. And His Airness could conceivably earn a nifty $20 million from those two projects alone. That's in addition to the estimated $40 million in product endorsement fees he raked in this year.

Jordan is arguably the most successful marketed athlete ever. Give Nike some credit for that. But some marketing experts suggest that Jordan's cheering section might be shrinking. And his latest leaps into Hollywood and the fragrance world are far from slam-dunks.

"There's only so far you can extend your celebrity," says Sam Craig, marketing department chairman at New York University. "After a while, you get into areas that dilute it."

Jordan's agent, David Falk, scoffs at such skepticism. "Five years ago some were saying that Michael had too many affiliations," says Falk. "They were wrong then, and they're wrong now. His popularity is unprecedented."

But there are warning signs that Jordan may

On Madison Ave.
By Bruce Horovitz

have lost a half-step in the endorsement arena. Especially among his core groupies: teens. Jordan isn't even the top-rated athlete among teens anymore, according to a survey of 1,000 teens released this month by the research firm Teenage Research Unlimited. In the firm's past two surveys, Orlando Magic basketball star Anfernee Hardaway has replaced Jordan in the top slot. "Michael's just not new anymore," says Maria Grossberg, who oversaw the survey.

But Bijan, the perfume magnate, says he expects to sell $60 million worth of Michael Jordan perfume its first year. That would rank it the biggest-ever first year for a new fragrance.

No chance, says Allan Mottus, a top fragrance industry consultant. Bijan is relying heavily upon sporting goods stores to sell the fragrance. "I wonder if the guy who walks in to buy a Chicago Bulls jacket really wants to buy a bottle of Michael Jordan cologne," Mottus says.

Then, there's the upcoming *Space Jam*, the live-action film with Jordan saving the animated Looney Toons characters from cartoon oblivion. Warner Bros.' ad chief Rob Friedman insists that *Space Jam* will be as big a hit as its wildly successful *Batman* and *Superman* films. At a cost of nearly $90 million to make, it'd better be.

McDonald's soon will be stuffing *Space Jam* toys into its Happy Meals. And Warner Bros. retail stores soon will be stuffed with *Space Jam* merchandise. But the movie is a question mark. "Michael Jordan is a proven licensing star," says Holly Sorensen, senior editor at *Premiere* magazine, "but he's not a proven movie star."

Celluloid hoopster: Jordan with co-star Bugs Bunny in Warner Bros.' movie 'Space Jam', which opens Nov. 15.

Chapter 13

Operating a Sports Marketing Firm

There are many different types of sports marketing firms, all with various specialties. Some firms strictly market athletes, while others measure sponsorship of advertising. In this day and age, with intense competition, it is important to specialize or be versatile, but the bottom line is results.

Businesses today aim to associate themselves with major sports. "Major sports" can refer to athletes, events, venues, or sports themes. At Sports Services of America™, we deal with corporate customers, meeting planners, PR firms, travel agents, marketing and advertising firms, Fortune 1,000 companies, tour companies, and incentive houses. The top reasons for my purchases are *premium* and *incentive* uses that motivate customers and employees.

Companies offer employees or customers rewards in exchange for making purchases or displaying good service or loyalty. A sports incentive program provides the intangibles that are associated with sports – *success, teamwork, family, and hard work.* Incentive programs reward *loyalty, team spirit, and hard work.*

Other *incentive programs* include game tickets to the nation's largest sporting events, cheerleader appearances, local team mascot appearances, golf outings with celebrities, "bat boy for a day" promotions, "caddie with pro for a day" promotions, competitions with athletes, chess with a favorite coach, long-distance shooting events, sports memorabilia giveaways, and practices with one's favorite player or team.

Organizing Sports-Related *Incentive Programs*

Business gifts and awards: Gifts to customers, stockholders, employees, or business friends to express appreciation.

Contests and sweepstakes: A contest is a competition based on skill in which prizes are offered. Proof of purchase is usually required with the entry. A candy bar wrapper with the opportunity to win a trip to the NBA All-Star game is an example. It gives a consumer incentive to choose that candy bar over its competitor.

A sweepstakes is a promotion which awards substantial prizes on the basis of a chance drawing. It is similar to a contest, but without the element of skill, and usually, for legal reasons, without "consideration." A person attending a card show keeps his ticket. A drawing offers attending members the chance to win sports memorabilia.

Dealer incentives: This one is given to a retailer with a specified purchase of one or more products, or for coupons or purchase credits accumulated over a period of time. A manufacturer might use this to reward his retail clients. This is a good way to maintain a good relationship between the manufacturer and retailer. Essentially, you are rewarding a client for loyalty and the dollar amount spent. Business-to-business currency transactions in America make up 50% of purchases, so it is important to reward the dealers.

Direct premiums: This is the simplest kind of premium – a situation in which an item is given free with a product at the time of the purchase. Examples include on-packs, in-packs, and container *premium*s as those given separately. Buy one box-seat ticket to the game and receive the second one at half-price.

In-packs and on-packs: The in-pack is a direct *premium* inside the pack. Autographed sports card in-packs are hot in the hobby market. An onpack is a direct *premium* attached to the exterior of a product or package, or sometimes riding in a special sleeve carton or film wrap.

Sales incentives: This awards a salesperson for achievements such as exceeding a quota, signing new accounts, reopening accounts, selling certain products, or achieving company objectives. An example of a sales incentive is awarding a salesperson All-Star Game tickets for selling the most products in a given time frame. Although it creates competition, it rewards success. If the employers simply offered cash, then employees may become dependent on such cash bonuses and feel at an emotional low when such bonuses do not occur.

Self liquidator: This device is a consumer *premium* (usually done by mail) for proof of purchase and a cash amount sufficient to cover the merchandise cost, plus shipping and handling. It may refer to any promotion in which the recipient pays the *premium* cost. Companies will put special cards inside packs that allow the consumer to receive an autograph. The consumer mails the special card back and pays for shipping and handling.

Traffic builders: A relatively low-cost *premium* offered free as an inducement to visit a store. A store logo T-shirt given to anyone coming to visit the store is one example. This *premium* is used to increase traffic and gain new customers (Association of Incentive Marketing).

Consulting Corporations On Sports Sponsorship

In 1995, it is estimated that 5,000 different companies invested over $4.5 billion in event sponsorship. Sponsored events can range from the X-Games to sports teams. Sports teams can include anything from baseball to mountain biking. Sponsorship in the last decade has become one of the hottest topics in the business. Stadiums are being promoted and sponsored at a breakneck pace. The Meadowlands facility, once known as the Brendan Byrne Arena, is now the Continental Airlines Arena. The client has the objective of getting more exposure for his or her company. Usually the client has a dollar figure he or she wants to spend. Some companies only sponsor local or regional events, while some sponsor worldwide events. I may look at upcoming sports events or related events and carefully advise my client as to what would benefit his/her company the most. I would also show the client how to monitor the contract between the sponsor and the sponsoree. The payment, performance, and terms stipulated in the contract play very important roles in sponsorship.

Consulting And Arranging Endorsements For Athletes And Companies

This is also a growing field. For example, Michael Jordan's endorsement figure alone is somewhere in the $40-million-a-year range. However, he is also the most high-profile athlete in the world. He endorses not just sports products such as Nike, but also non-sports services like LDDS long distance. The use of athletes to represent non-sports merchandise and services will increase as businesses branch into the sports arena. Marketing firms can represent many athletes from different walks of life and with different images, both public and personal. Sports marketing firms look to capitalize on matching businesses with athletes based on shared images and objectives. Endorsement opportunities can be financially rewarding to an athlete and the representing company.

Arranging Athlete Appearances For Advertising, Promotion, Grand Openings, And Speaking Engagements.

These are considered "live events." In marketing, this means the athlete must be there at a certain time to promote the product or service. In advertising it relates to both television and print advertising. Promotion means a specific product or service that requires the athlete to appear "live." This is important to maintain good relationships with athletes and clients.

Operating A Speaker's Bureau

In operating a full-service speaker's bureau, I meet with a planner or a human-resource executive of a company. I find out what type of motivational speech the company is looking for and inquire about the budget, location, and time. I then look at who I have available to fill their need and fax a list of candidates within the hour.

Because of the competition between bureaus, representatives work together to expand athlete portfolios. Sports marketing firms are aggressive. A hefty percentage of the quoted fees, usually 20% to 33%, often goes to the agent. It is important to book speakers as exclusive clients. However, when an exclusive contract is signed by the athlete, the marketing company absorbs all promotional costs (this usually includes a $10-$25 press kit) and manages the paperwork. Most speakers remain independent, though.

Certain businesses associate themselves with major sports activities and athletes who are symbols of goodwill. Marketing agencies work with meeting planners, human resources departments, PR firms, travel agents, marketing agencies, advertising firms, Fortune 1000 companies, tour companies, and incentive houses. The majority of athlete requests for speaking engagements are based on motivation, giveaways, and sales promotions.

Sports marketing companies often develop giveaways that offer people opportunities to win Super Bowl trips. One particular program was conducted at a major appliance store that sold different brands. With this program, the company found that the store sold its employees brands that provided a chance to win the trip 100 times more than normal. The association with the Super Bowl was not bad for the product, either.

Some marketing companies have access to more than 1,000 of the world's greatest athletes, whether from basketball, baseball, football, tennis, golf, cycling, swimming, gymnastics, or golf. With a celebrity sports star, you'll get the winning spokesperson in advertising, corporate outings, sales meetings, and more.

Favorite Reasons Companies Choose Sports
1. Gain high visibility to a target consumer group.
2. Associate products with values such as fitness and excellence.
3. Convey a positive image of company/product
4. Motivate sales staff with event perks.
5. Create brand image.

NFL Football	51%
MLB Baseball	21%
NBA Basketball	18%
NHL Hockey	7%
no preference	3%
	100%

<u>*Favorite Professional Teams*</u>

Dallas Cowboys	28%
Chicago Bulls	14%
San Francisco 49ers	12%
Atlanta Braves	10%
New York Giants	6%
Washington Redskins	6%
Miami Dolphins	6%
Kansas City Chiefs	6%
Buffalo Bills	6%
Oakland Raiders	<u>6%</u>
	100%

Sample And Costs Of Sports Promotions

(Sports Services of America™)

* Football (promotion special):	* Baseball (promotion special):
Reserve: $4,250	Reserve: $4,750
Starter: $5,000	Starter: $5,500
Pro Bowl Player: $11,500	All-Star Player: $11,500
Retired Player: $4,000	Retired Player: $4,000
Hall of Fame Player: $9,500	Hall of Fame Player: $9,500
* Basketball (promotion special):	* Hockey (promotion special):
Reserve: $4,250	Reserve: $4,250 promotion
Starter: $8,500	Starter: $6,000
All Star Player: $16,000	All Star Player: $11,500
Retired Player: $5,000*	Retired Player: $4,000
Hall of Fame Player: $10,500	Hall of Fame Player: $8,500

* Football Hall of Fame (promotion special):	* Baseball Fantasy (promotion special):
Five Football Heroes or Hall of Fame-Caliber Players: $15,000	Five Baseball Heroes or Hall of Fame-Caliber Players: $20,000
* Team Cheerleaders (promotion special) $500 for 2 in full costume	

Types Of Promotions Sports Marketing Firms Offer

* Promotion Special: This sports promotion is a talent evaluation for promotional purposes. It includes the services of our professional PR department with 100 media contacts, 50 officially licensed photos, and two-hour appearances with a professional celebrity talent.

Grand Slam Sports Promotion: This sports promotion is a talent evaluation for promotional purposes and includes the services of our professional PR department with 200 media contacts, 400 officially licensed photos, four-hour limousine service available to the talent, two Sports Services of America trained professional celebrity talent coordinators, a 10x10 booth set up on-site, poster signage consultation, appropriate advertisement, and four print displays or four radio announcements, or point-of-purchase display consultation and coordination.

Speech Topics Offered with Sample Order Form

❏ Advertising

❏ Aging / Retirement

❏ Arts / Culture / Music

❏ Athletics / Sports

❏ Assertiveness

❏ Body Language

❏ Business

❏ Development

❏ Change

❏ Character Portrayals

❏ Communication Skills

❏ Creativity

❏ Crisis Management

❏ Cross Cultural Training

❏ Customer Service

❏ Cyberspace

❏ Decision Making

❏ Delegation Skills

❏ Disaster Management

❏ Diversity

❏ Drug Abuse

❏ Economics

❏ Management by Objectives

❏ Managerial Competencies

❏ Communications

❏ Marketing Management

❏ Media Relations

❏ Memory

❏ Merchandising

❏ Morals

❏ Motivation

❏ Negotiation Skills

❏ Networking

❏ Nutrition

❏ Organizational Skills

❏ Patriotic

❏ Performance Improvement

❏ Planning Skills

❏ Presentation Skills

❏ Persuasion Skills

❏ Politics

❏ Presentation Skills

❏ Problem Solving

❏ Productivity Improvement

- Education
- Empowerment
- Environmental
- Ethics
- Etiquette
- Family
- Financial
- Fitness
- Future
- Goal Setting
- Harassment
- Health
- Humor
- Image / Dressing
- Innovation
- International Affairs
- Internet (World Wide Web)
- Law
- Leadership Development
- Learning to Organize
- Learning-to-Learn
- Listening Skills
- Magic
- Management Skills
- Management Development

- Psychology
- Public Relations
- Reading Skills
- Relationships
- Retirement
- Safety
- Sales Force Motivation
- Sales Skills
- Self-esteem Services
- Supervisory Skills
- Sports
- Strategic Planning
- Stress Management
- Substance Abuse
- Team Building
- Technology
- Telephone Skills
- Time Management
- Training
- Trends
- Wellness
- Women in Society
- Writing Skills
- Other

Team: _____

Players:

1st choice _____ Quote $ _____

2nd choice _____ Quote $_____

3rd choice _____ Quote $ _____

- For specific talent requests, a non-refundable negotiation fee or deposit may be required.

Appearance *(information must be completed or fee may be implemented):*

Month: _____

Day: _____

Time: _____

Address: _____

Phone: _____

This Agreement is made between COMPANY and ADDRESS _____,
hereinafter referred to as "COMPANY." Whereas SSA is a representative for the negotiations and
scheduling of _____, a professional athlete, hereinafter referred to as
"ATHLETE"; and whereas, COMPANY desires to schedule a personal appearance by ATHLETE,
COMPANY and SSA agree to the personal appearance and autograph-signing session of
ATHLETE for the following:

COMPANY agrees to pay SSA the full compensation $_____ for ATHLETE's
appearance and signing. Additionally, COMPANY agrees to provide transportation for
ATHLETE's travel to and from the show, if needed. ATHLETE agrees to permit COMPANY to
use his name and likeness in the promotion, advertising and pre-sale of this personal appearance. In
the event that COMPANY cancels this appearance or show, it is agreed that any deposits or
payments made are forfeited and non-refundable. In the unlikely event ATHLETE cancels this
appearance due to extreme illness or other unforeseen cause, it is agreed that any deposits made
will be refunded in full or the appearance will be rescheduled.

All parties agree to indemnify and hold each other, along with their principals, agents, and
representatives, harmless from and against any and all claims, demands, losses, damages, liabilities,
costs, fines, expenses, and penalties resulting from any claims, proceedings, or actions arising out
of or in conjunction with a breach of any provision of this agreement by the other party.

Signed and Agreed upon by:

_____

Please send check to:

Sports Services of America
333 Washington Blvd., Suite 360
Marina Del Rey, CA 90292

This is a service provided by Sports Services of America™ and a fee has been attached to each price. **Sample of what a Super Bowl ticket would cost. A fee is associated with the service of obtaining the ticket from a service such as Sports Services of America™.**

SUPER BOWL

LOCATION: NEW ORLEANS

DATE: JANUARY 26, 1997

LOCATION	SECTION	PRICE
End Zone		
Upper:	623-631 & 605-649	$1,100 (fee incl.)
Plaza:	319-329 & 305-343	$1,250 (fee incl.)
Lower:	125-131 & 103-152	$1,250 (fee incl.)
Corner		
Upper:	633-635 & 645-647	$1,200 (fee incl.)
	621-619 & 609-607	
Plaza:	331, 341, 305, 307 &	$1,300 (fee incl.)
Lower:	317	$1,450 (fee incl.)
	132, 128 & 134, 136 & 148, 150 & 108, 106	

Goal Line - 20 yard.		
Upper:	637, 643, 61 & 617	$1,300 (fee incl.)
Plaza:	315, 309, 339 & 333	$1,800 (fee incl.)
Lower:	118, 110, 146 & 138	$1,900 (fee incl.)

20 yard - 20 yard		
Upper:	639, 641 & 615, 613	$1,700 (fee incl.)
Plaza:	334-339 & 309-313	$1,900 (fee incl.)
Lower:	118-110 & 138-146	$2,750 (fee incl.)

Football Package price includes Super Bowl ticket (fee)

HOTEL NEW ORLEANS

NEW ORLEANS, LOUISIANA

January 23-27, 1997

- 5 days/4 nights deluxe accommodations at the Hotel New Orleans, conveniently located in the historic warehouse district and the world-famous Riverwalk and French Quarter

- Full American breakfast daily
- Game day brunch with live jazz .

- Cocktail party featuring a celebrity guest speaker
- Super Bowl reserved game ticket
- Transportation to and from the game
- Deluxe package of Super Bowl gifts and amenities
- All taxes and gratuities

Single	$4,049	Double	$3,240
Triple	3,029	Quad:	2,921

When putting packages together and selling tickets, customers have the use of diagrams to determine where the best seats are located. Pricing is determined by location. Below is a diagram that accompanies the 1996 All-Star Game.

1996 Baseball Package (Includes All-Star Game Tickets Fee.)

PLACE: PHILADELPHIA

LOCATION	PRICE
FIELD BOX	
Between Bases:	$ 950.00 (fee include)
Inside Foul Pole:	$ 600.00
CLUB BOX	
Between Bases:	$ 750.00
Inside Foul Pole:	$ 550.00

UPPERBOX

Between Bases:	$ 450.00
Inside Foul Pole:	$ 350.00

OUTFIELD

Upper Rows:	$ 250.00
Lower Rows:	$ 300.00

More Great Products And Services For Future Sports Marketers!

☐   Earn 10% for booking Kermit Pemberton to speak at your
next meeting.   Price: quote

☐   Game Tickets to all major sporting events.   Price: quote

☐   Sports Celebrity Appearances and Publicity. Price: quote

☐   Sports Marketing Video #1010   Price: $49.95

☐   How to use sports celebrities to endorse products and
services. Video #1019   Price: $49.95

☐   Game Tickets and Hospitality used to motivate customers
and employees. Video #1019   Price: $49.95

☐   How to create media attention with your next promotion or
special event with the use of sports celebrities tape. #1011
                              Price: $49.95

☐   Sports Services of America: Baseball Cap "Pro-Style"
#1013   Price: $14.95

☐   The Money Side of Sports: Baseball Cap "Pro-Style" #1014
                              Price: $14.95

Sports Service of America Publishing™
333 Washington Blvd., Suite 360
Marina Del Rey, CA 90292

Visa/MasterCard orders call:

(310) 821-4490 or FAX (310) 821-0522

My Inspiration

The story of my grandfather, as told by my mother, reminds me of a different time. In this fast-paced society of electronics, what gets lost is the importance of knowing your customer, which is the basis of marketing. Knowing your customer is more than a phone call; it is an action. The days of deals on a handshake seem well behind us. We get lost in our day-to-day jobs and sometimes don't remember that it's our customers who keep us in business.

When we deal with athletes, they sometimes seem to have a pulse on society. As a marketer, I try to understand the electricity and presence an athlete can bring. My grandfather understood not only marketing, but the importance of the one-on-one relationship that must occur to create a successful business. I am grateful that I have had the opportunity to have my own business and to be associated with sports. Nearly 50 years ago, my grandfather knew success was based on relationships. Taking the time to cultivate and build relationships is what it's all about. Sports marketing is driven by association and honor. My grandfather understood all of this well before the electronic age. One-on-one service and success go hand in hand.

In 1948, my grandfather, Wayne Chapman, began his first business venture. The eldest of 17 children, he started a sit-down barbecue restaurant in his hometown, Owensboro, Ken. Although

Owensboro was a predominately black community, the schools and churches had a racially mixed attendance. Here Grandfather Wayne's restaurant prospered.

In 1951, Grandfather Wayne made a daring business move that few of his color in the area had previously attempted. He decided to move his restaurant across town, just beyond the railroad tracks. He envisioned market potential where others saw only risk and uncertainty. For Grandfather Wayne, this new business environment was an opportunity for him to achieve the American dream.

He knew he could apply the same business principles of high-quality food and customer service across town when he dealt with upper-middle-class clients as he did with his existing clients.

He purchased his meat from Fields Packing House, widely known for its choice meats, and he served only the best product at a fair price! Sometimes he would include extras such as fresh potato salad where his competitors would not. He was always looking for new ways to attract additional business.

My grandfather understood the importance of good customer service. It was as important as good food. Any time my grandfather was in the restaurant, he would ask each customer, "How's the meal? Is the service OK?" That's the way it was; business was serious. My grandfather took every customer's complaint and comment seriously, even adjusting the price of a meal when a client felt it was too high. He knew how to make the customer feel welcome and satisfied.

The importance of an open mind

Wayne got to know his customers and fellow businessmen in this new business environment, sometimes inviting them into his home for dinner.

This new group of businessmen entered through the kitchen. This was a show of respect and acceptance for a colored man. These men were big-business men in a time when a few businessmen ran an entire community.

They taught my grandfather some principles and proper procedures of doing business in this small town, which he applied to his business environment. As they taught him how their businesses functioned, he was able to make revisions and use their sound, tried-and-true practices to achieve success in his business. He was always very eager to learn and was constantly canvassing the public he served to improve both the quantity and quality of service.

The big businessmen from the other side of the tracks were also able to learn from him and save a little money on services he provided; it was a mutual exchange, and both parties benefited from the relationship – in many cases serving the same clients.

By the middle of 1953, meat became too expensive and his profit began to shrink for the take-out barbecue pit. Networking and a solid reputation based on honesty, customer relations, and integrity allowed him to begin a new business.

Marketing and public relations the way my grandfather did it.

Due to the price increase of meat, he realized he could no longer stay in business and make a profit. He began selling fresh fruit door-to-door. This approach allowed him to know his customers and their needs. Their eyes would glow when they peered at the fresh fruit on the very same truck it had been placed on after it had been plucked. He also added charm by saying, "Oh, what a handsome young man you are!" to the customer's son, or "Would this apple make you stop crying, young lady?" to the customer's young daughter. He was more than a fruit seller; he was a friend. My grandfather got to know his customers better by going door-to-door.

Understanding and caring about his customers helped him understand supply and demand. The fruit business was different because fruit was perishable. Unsold fruit went against profit, and he had a family to feed. My grandfather knew that Ms. Lilly baked 30 apple pies every other week to sell at her bakery, and she needed 300 Washington State apples for her pies. Ms. Lilly's apples had to be from Washington, and if they were not right, she would not buy. He knew what his customers required on both sides of the tracks. Business was booming because of good service and timely deliveries. He was able to feed his family of nine and also purchase new trucks and a home using these principles of marketing.

The importance of an open mind, networking, a good product, marketing, public relations, and understanding customers' needs.

Marketing firms cannot afford to go door-to-door to sell their services, but what applied to my grandfather applies to business today. Honesty and integrity – taking the time to know your customer's needs – come first and foremost. Time and technology change the way we do business. In the electronic age, we lose out on personal relationships and building trust and loyalty. My grandfather understood the importance of personal service. That was the key to his success. Using sports celebrities and game tickets is now the American way of sharing a bond or common ground (Increasingly, it is the *global* way of sharing common ground, with American sports being promoted throughout the world.) Sports marketing is now the means by which companies build personal relations, trust, loyalty, and bonds of association.

Glossary

Association: A connection, combination, or relationship of ideals, feelings, or sensations.

Athlete: An athlete is PR. An athlete spreads the goodwill of sports in the public's eyes. Most of an athlete's goodwill is based on how well he performs on the field of battle, and the remainder is based on his relations with the public.

Business Gifts and Awards: Gifts to customers, stockholders, employees, or business friends used to express appreciation.

Bond: Something that binds a person or persons to a certain circumstance or behaviors.

Contests and Sweepstakes: Contests are competitions based on skills in which prizes are offered. A proof of purchase is usually required with entry. A candy bar wrapper with the opportunity to win a trip to the NBA All-Star Game is one example. It gives consumers an incentive to choose that candy bar over a competitor. Sweepstakes are promotions that award substantial prizes on the basis of chance drawings. Sweepstakes are similar to contests, but without the element of skill – and usually, for legal reasons, without "consideration." A person attending a card show keeps his ticket. A drawing offers attending members the chance to win sports memorabilia.

Contract: Legal, signed papers specifying payment, performance, and terms.

Customer: The person who purchases goods or services from another.

Demographic: Statistical data about a population that shows average age, income, education, gender, or ethnic makeup.

Dealer Incentives: An incentive given to a retailer with a specified purchase of one or more products, or for coupons or purchase credits accumulated over a period of time. A manufacturer might use this to reward his retail clients. This is a good way to maintain a positive relationship between the manufacturer and retailer. Essentially, you are rewarding a client for loyalty and the dollar amount spent, providing an added incentive to maintain a good business relationship.

Direct Premium: The simplest kind of premium – when an item is given free with a product at the time of the purchase. Examples include on-packs and in-packs. Buy one box-seat ticket to the game receive the second one at half-price.

Emotional appeals: Message appeals that attempt to arouse negative or positive emotions that will motivate purchase. Examples include fear, guilt, shame, love, humor, pride, and joy appeals.

Endorsee: The company that represents and produces the product or products that are being endorsed.

Endorsement: To express approval or support publicly. To designate oneself as payee of a check by signing. The purpose of assigning one's interest therein to another. To make good on an item. When an athlete signs a letter of endorsement with an endorsee, he becomes a business partner of the endorsee. The athlete is signing his name on someone else's check; therefore, the athlete should make sure the funds are in the bank.

Entertainment: Diversion, amusement, affording pleasure. Light in nature. Gross Impression: The number of impressions made by associating a product or service with an athlete, team, or sport.

Events: Happenings staged to communicate messages to target audiences, such as news conferences and grand openings.

Intangible: Not material. Something that cannot be defined by specific words.

Integrity: Uncompromising adherence to moral and ethical principles and complete soundness of moral character.

In-pack and On-pack: The in-pack is a direct premium inside the package. Autographed cards inside packs are hot in the hobby market. An on-pack is a direct premium attached to the exterior of a product or package, or sometimes riding in a special sleeve carton or film wrap.

Licensing Agreement: A license agreement is a granting or giving of rights to use a name, image, logo, or likeness. *By Claire D. Moomjian*

Loyalty: A feeling of faithfulness or allegiance.

Marketing: The process used to relate a product or service to consumers. *By Scott Williams*

Marketing Mix: The set of controllable marketing variables a firm blends to produce the response it wants in the target market.

Media Impact: The qualitative value of an exposure through a given medium.

Media Vehicles: Specific media, such as specific magazines, television shows, or radio programs.

Need: A situation of difficulty.

Networking: The breaking of bread. To share the same common experience. To find common ground. Any way one can share the same feeling and feel relaxed. Example: taking a client to a sporting event or meeting a sports celebrity.

News: A report of a recent event. Information reported.

Owner: The sole agent of sports activities or actions. (Persons cannot be owned.)

Perception: The process by which people select, organize, and interpret information to form a meaningful picture of the world.

Personal Influence: The effect of statements made by one person upon another person's attitudes or likeliness to purchase.

Premiums: Goods offered either free or at a low cost as an incentive to buy a product.

Product: An item produced by labor.

Product Image: The way consumers perceive an actual or potential product.

Promoter: A person or thing that promotes, furthers, encourages.   A person who organizes and finances a sporting event.

Promotion: The publicizing or advertising of a product.

Psychographics: The technique of measuring lifestyles and developing life-style classifications. It involves measuring the major AIO dimensions (activities, interests, opinions).

Public: The population or community.

Publicize: To bring to the public's notice.

Publicly: In a public or open manner or place.

Public Relations: The spreading of goodwill in the public's eyes.

Pull Strategy: A promotional strategy that calls for spending a lot of money on advertising and consumer promotion to build up consumer demand. If it is successful, consumers will ask their retailers for the product. The retailer will ask the wholesalers and the wholesalers will ask the producers.

Push Strategy: A promotional strategy that uses the sales force and trade promotion to push the product through channels. Producers promote the product to wholesalers, wholesalers promote to retailers, and retailers promote to consumers.

Reach: The percentage of people in the target market exposed to an ad campaign during a given period of time.

Retailing: Selling goods or services directly to final consumers for their personal, non-business use.

Sales Incentives: This awards a sales person for achievements such as exceeding a sales quota, signing new accounts, reopening accounts, selling certain products, or achieving company objectives. An example of this is awarding a salesperson All-Star Game tickets for selling the most product in a given time frame. It creates competition and rewards success.

Segmentation: Dividing the market into groups based on demographic variables such as age, sex, family size, family life cycle, income, occupation, education, religion, race, and nationality.

Self Liquidator: A consumer premium (usually by mail) for proof of purchase and a cash amount sufficient to cover the merchandise cost, plus shipping and handling. May refer to any promotion in which recipient pays the premium cost. In the hobby industry, companies will put special sports cards inside packs, allowing consumers to receive an autograph if they mail the special card and pay for shipping and handling.

Sell-out: A feeling in the air, the noise, smell of peanuts, beer breath, and a shaking sense of being a part of something special.

Sport: The product of goodwill, hard work, effort, sincerity, loss, gain, and struggle. Something everyone can identify with. Sports is like a rock in the business world, it does nothing without the athlete – the ambassador and promoter of a sport.

Sports Broadcasting: To transmit sports programs from a radio or television station. To speak, perform, or present on a radio or television program regarding sports. Sports radio or television is a business profession. The act of transmitting entertainment by radio or television – this is a business.

Sports Marketing: The buying or selling in the sports market.

Sports Market Research: The gathering and studying of data in the sports industry.

Sports Merchandise: Sporting goods that are bought and sold.

Success: Overcoming obstacles with a favorable outcome.

Survey Research: Gathering of primary data by asking people questions about their knowledge, attitudes, preferences, and buying behavior.

Teamwork: A cooperative effort on the part of a group of persons acting together in the interest of a common cause.

Trade Promotion: Sales promotion designed to motivate reseller support and to improve reseller selling efforts, including discounts, allowances, free goods, cooperative advertising, push money, conventions, and trade shows.

Traffic Builders: A relatively low-cost premium offered free as an inducement to visit a store. A store logo T-shirt given to anyone coming to visit the store is an example. This premium is used to increase traffic and gain new customers. (Association of Incentive Marketing)

Trust: Reliance on the integrity, strength, ability, and surety of a person or thing. Complete confidence.

Winning: Finishing first in a contest.

Word-of-Mouth Influence: Personal communication about a product between specific buyers and neighbors, friends, family members, and associates.

Work Ethic: A moral belief in the importance of work and its inherent ability to strengthen character.

More Great Products And Services For Future Sports Marketers!

☐   Earn 10% for booking Kermit Pemberton to speak at your next meeting.   Price: quote

☐   Game Tickets to all major sporting events.   Price: quote

☐   Sports Celebrity Appearances and Publicity. Price: quote

☐   Sports Marketing Video #1010   Price: $49.95

☐   How to use sports celebrities to endorse products and services. Video #1019   Price: $49.95

☐   Game Tickets and Hospitality used to motivate customers and employees. Video #1019   Price: $49.95

☐   How to create media attention with your next promotion or special event with the use of sports celebrities tape. #1011
                                           Price: $49.95

☐   Sports Services of America: Baseball Cap "Pro-Style" #1013   Price: $14.95

☐   The Money Side of Sports: Baseball Cap "Pro-Style" #1014   Price: $14.95

Sports Service of America Publishing™
333 Washington Blvd., Suite 360
Marina Del Rey, CA 90292

Visa/MasterCard orders call:

(310) 821-4490 or FAX (310) 821-0522